WITNESS

A Story of Survival and Triumph

by Mendel Tessler

as told to Shaindy Perl

INTRODUCTION

"When Pharaoh restored the chief butler to his position as foretold by Joseph in his interpretation of the butler's dream, he forgot Joseph. 'Yet the chief butler did not remember Joseph but forgot him.' Why does the Bible use this repetitive language? It is obvious that if the butler forgot Joseph, he did not remember him. Yet both verbs are used, 'not remembering' and 'forgetting.' The Torah, in using this language, is teaching us a very important lesson. There are events of such overbearing magnitude that one ought not to remember them all the time, but one must not forget them either. Such an event is the Holocaust"

– Rabbi Israel Spira, the Duzhov-Bluzhover Rebbe, a survivor

When Simon Dubnow, the famous octogenarian Jewish historian who was shot by a former gentile student, shouted his final words *Yidn, shreibt un fershreibt!"*, Yiddish for, "Jews, write and record!", he was expressing the most common anxiety of all Holocaust victims, that they and their families never be forgotten.

But for the vast majority of survivors, the *Shearit Hapletah*, "Remnants of the Remnants," it was near impossible to put pen to paper. The most deafening post-Holocaust sound was the silence. Most wanted desperately to tell the world what had happened. "I will survive to tell the story!" was a common determined defiant. Of course most never made it. Their memories and dreams and hopes died with them at Auschwitz or Treblinka.

Among those to whom God had granted the gift of (more) life there were few with the emotional stamina and the skills to do so. And for others, since "It" made no sense, there was no sense writing about it; and more: the few publishers who were interested faced an insurmountable challenge: most readers, no matter how well-intentioned and empathetic, simply had no capacity to grasp what they were being told.

Many of the survivors, lonely and alone, scarred and scared, confused and traumatized, remained haunted for years. Some for decades. This was a vicious literary Catch-22: A dam of ever-rising speechlessness waiting to burst. The inability to write only intensified the survivor's sense of isolation. Most were preoccupied trying to create new lives, new families, jobs, languages, even new type of gentile neighbors. With time, the tattoos faded, the skin grew old. Nobody paid much attention to them. At first, in the Orthodox Jewish community, only a handful of memoirs appeared after the war ended and the ovens switched off in early 1945. *But...*

Eventually the human need to share experiences broke through the hushed stillness. For to forget is to kill twice. This is why R' Mendel Tessler's work, *Witness: A Story Of Survival and Triumph,* is so important. Feeling a keen sense of history on his shoulders to act as a link with the past and preserve the way of life of European Torah Jewry as a role model to children, grandchildren and great-grandchildren, his is a significant contribution to Orthodox Holocaust literature.

R' Tessler's account of his childhood in Vişeu de Sus, Maramureş County, Romania, the deportations, the Dante's hell at Auschwitz-Birkenau, the lethal death march, the unbearable losses, the incomprehensible survival, the stay in the sprawling Feldafing DP camp in Moravia, the adjustment to a western culture – and the success in raising a *frum* family is nothing short of breathtaking. It is a vehicle of triumphism over Hitlerism.

"Paper survives," noted Rabbi Dr. Jacob Avigdor, the chief rabbi of Drohobych and one of the few Polisher rabbis to survive, "a person and his memories die. But the book remains". This manuscript will be read for generations. A *yosher koach* to R' Mendel Tessler!

Joe Bobker
Lawrence, LI, NY
Shavuos 2017

DEDICATION

I BELIEVE THAT everything that I was able to accomplish in my life is thanks to the upbringing I received in the home of my father and mother before the war and to the devotion my father showed me afterwards. My parents gave us children a foundation of security and deep faith and the values they instilled in us enabled us to remain strong.

During the war, my father lost his wife, who was thirty-nine when she was murdered, and six little children, between the ages of four and twelve. Nonetheless he cared for me after I was injured without a word of complaint and without mentioning his own suffering. He accepted all that had happened as having been decreed *Min HaShomayim*, with no questions. His inner strength and unwavering faith, despite all he went through, gave us surviving sons the courage to go on. The keen intelligence with which he related to us was profound, and I will remember forever how he cared for me with steady devotion.

Once I was ready to settle down and establish a family of my own, I was blessed to marry my beloved wife and life partner, Nusia. Nusia and I worked tirelessly side by side to raise our children, our precious "flowers". Nothing was more important to Nusia than our children, and she dedicated herself completely to their welfare. In every situation, my children and I could count on her wisdom and wit, and nothing ever stood in the way of Nusia's fierce love for her family. I am reminded of Nusia's passionate battle cry, "*Alles far de kinder!*" each time I am surrounded by my children and their families, and I know she is still watching over us all and shepping continued Nachas from our dear children and grandchildren.

Teiere Tatte and *Mamme*, dearest Nusia, thank you for making my journey possible.

"קטנתי מכל החסדים ומכל האמת אשר
עשית את עבדך כי במקלי עברתי את הירדן
הזה ועתה הייתי לשני מחנות."

(בראשית לב:יא)

"I have become small from all the kindness
and all the faithfulness that You have rendered
to Your servant for with my staff I crossed this
Yarden, and now I have become two camps."

*Katonti—I was small, just a young boy—when I merited
Your kindness and faithfulness. With my staff—the
crutches I needed to support myself after my injury—I
crossed the ocean, and now, Hashem in His mercy, has
helped me become multiple camps, as I have been blessed
with children, grandchildren, and great-grandchildren.*

– Mendel Tessler

TABLE OF CONTENTS

CHAPTER ONE:
ONCE UPON A TOWN

I was born on 18 Elul, 5689, or September 23, 1929,[1] in Vişeu de Sus in Maramureş County, a beautiful mountainous area in northern Romania. We Jews referred to our town as Visheve and the region as Marmorosh.

Visheve actually consists of three connected towns: Upper, Middle, and Lower Visheve. We referred to them in Yiddish as Oyber-Visheve (Vişeu de Sus), Mittel-Visheve (Vişeu de Mijloc), and Inter-Visheve (Vişeu de Jos). These towns are often referred to collectively as "the Visheves." My family lived at the very edge of the Jewish section of Oyber-Visheve, near the Viseu River, which flowed through the town and played an important role in the region's economy.

Our town was fairly large, with many stores and even a hospital. There were about 15,000 residents in all, and they were about equally divided into three main groups: Jews, Germans, and Romanians. The closest city to the Visheves is the city of Sighet, which is about

---

1   For many years, I used November 23, 1929, as my birth date. I knew I was born on Chai Elul, a day that cannot possibly fall on November 23; however, November 23 was the official birthday on all my legal documents. I believe this discrepancy happened because the magistrate visited towns periodically and recorded all new births on the date of his visit.

     Much later, after my father's Mishnayos was returned to Naftuli (see Chapter 14), we found the Hebrew and Gregorian birthdates of all my siblings, listed on the very first page. That discovery finally set the record straight: I was born on September 23, not November 23. Nonetheless, I continued using the November date as my birthday, since I was already accustomed to doing so and it was the date that appeared on all important documents.

forty-eight kilometers (thirty miles) away and also had a large Jewish community at that time.

My father, Shlomo Tessler, was born to Mottel and Fradel Tessler, who also lived in our town. However, when my father was born in 1898, the Visheves were part of Austria-Hungary. After World War I, Maramures was divided between Romania and Czechoslovakia, and the town became part of Romania. The Visheves are still part of Romania today, though for a brief period between 1940 and 1944, it was annexed to Hungary.

My father came from a large family of ten children: eight boys and two girls. Five of his older brothers immigrated to the United States at the turn of the century, though one, Mendel, ultimately returned to Romania. After his return, Mendel married a local girl, Rachel, and had five daughters, but he passed away when they were still young. I was born shortly afterwards and am named after him. My middle name, Ber, is after a sixth brother, Berel, who passed away while serving in the army during World War I. My father and his youngest brother Baruch remained in Visheve and both established families there. Their two sisters lived in nearby towns: Faiga, who had married Yitzchok Yaakov Fireworker, lived in Moisei (or Mesiv, in Yiddish), and Yenta, who had married Shlomo Mendelovitch, lived in Borsa. Faiga was much older than my father, and her oldest daughter, Ekka, married Baruch, Ekka's uncle.

My mother, Esther Tessler, was born in Vilchovitz, Czechoslovakia, to her parents Shmiel Chaim and Golda Rosenfeld. Vilchovitz is also part of the Maramures region of the Carpathian Mountains and is actually quite close to the Visheves. However, it became part of Czechoslovakia when the region was split into different countries, following the defeat of the Austro-Hungarian Empire.

My mother came from a family of eleven children. Tragically, her mother and five siblings all passed away in one week, during an epidemic between 1918 and 1920. She survived together with three sisters, Sheindel, Udel, and Genendel, and two brothers, Leibish (who was the mayor of Vilchovitz) and Yitzchok Dovid.

Both Visheve and Vilchovitz contained large Vizhnitz communities. In fact, the Kosov-Vizhnitz dynasty originated in Marmorosh from the days of the Baal Shem Tov, when he sent his holy *chassid*, Reb Yaakov Koppel Chossid, to the region. Reb Yaakov was from the town of Kolomaye, and for many years he had a small wood and textile store there. Though he lived as a simple Jew, the Baal Shem Tov recognized his true greatness and appointed him as the *shaliach tzibbur* whenever Reb Yaakov Koppel came to Mezbizh. One day, the Baal Shem Tov called him over and pointed to the region of Marmorosh. "This is a beautiful flower garden," the Rebbe said. "I want you to take care of it." Though Reb Yaakov Koppel never became a *rebbe* himself, he brought *chassidus* to Marmorosh and was the father of the Kosov-Vizhnitz dynasty.

Now, more than 150 years later, the Ahavas Yisrael of Vizhnitz led the *chassidus* from Grosswardein, Romania. His eldest son, Reb Menachem Mendel Hager, the Sheiris Menachem, was the Vishever Rav. The Rebbe's second son, Rav Chaim Meir Hager, was the Vilchovitzer Rav, leading the community where my maternal grandparents lived.[2]

Life in Visheve was simple and pleasant. There was a large Jewish presence, with close to 5,000 Jewish residents. They were all warm, *chassidishe* people, who spoke Yiddish as their first language. The men wore traditional long *kapotas* (overcoats) or *kurtze reklech* (short jackets) and had long beards. Some more modern Jewish men had *geshtitzte berd* (trimmed beards). The women wore dresses that had long sleeves and reached well below their knees. They wore *tichelech* over their heads and tied them under their chins. Some modern women tied their *tichelech* at the nape of their necks. For Shabbos and *simchos,* the women wore *sheitels*.

---

2   In Sivan 1936, after the passing of the Ahavas Yisrael, the Vilchovitzer Rav, who later became known as the Imrei Chaim of Vizhnitz, took his father's place as the head of the *chassidus,* as his older brother, the Sheiris Menachem, was in America at the time for an extended fund-raising trip.

Torah and *chassidus* were at the center of Jewish life, and several *chassidic* dynasties were represented in the Visheves, including Vizhnitz, Sighet (Satmar), Spink, Rachov, and Kretchnif. Though my paternal grandfather, Mottel Tessler, had been a Spinke *chassid*, both my father and maternal grandfather, the distinguished *chassid* Reb Shmiel Chaim Rosenfeld, were prominent Vizhnitz *chassidim*. Thus, we were part of the close-knit Vizhnitz community of the Visheves and the *chassidus* played an important role in my family's life.

The Vishever *kehillah* was well-organized with all the institutions of a large Jewish community. There were twelve *shuls,* a *yeshiva,* as well as a Talmud Torah, *matzah* bakery, and *mikvah.* A *kehillah* tax, which we called *gebela,* was included in the cost of a *shechitah* ticket, and added to items like *heiven* (yeast). The money collected supported the Rav and all the *kehillah* institutions.

Hashgachah for *shechitah* in the Visheves was very strict. The Talmud Torah and *matzah* bakery were next to each other on the Yiddishe Gas (the Jewish Street), and at the same location, there was a row of butcher stands housed inside a large building where local butchers rented space from the *kehillah.* The *mashgiach* had the keys to the building at all times and was the one to open and close it each day. When the meat was transported from the slaughterhouse to the butcher stands, the *mashgiach* rode in a horse-drawn wagon together with the meat. Under his watchful eye, the meat was distributed to the butchers, who then sold it to their customers. The local housewives would buy the meat and *kasher* it on their own.

A different system was used to slaughter birds, like chicken, geese, ducks and turkeys. These, most townspeople raised on their own. We would buy a *shechitah* ticket, which came in different colors, one for each type of bird. Then, we would bring the bird and ticket to the *shochet*'s home. Sometimes the Shochet'ke, as we called the wife, would instruct us to come back later, but if the *shochet* was available, he would *shecht* it on the spot. Transporting chickens to and from the *shochet* was a typical errand that we children did regularly. On rare occasions, when we needed several birds slaughtered at once, the *shochet* would be called to come to our home instead.

Another *kehillah* service was Shabbos *tzetlach* that were distributed by the *shamash* each Thursday. This was a one-week calendar page that had the name of the *sedrah*, all the *z'manim*, and any other relevant information printed on it.

Most of Visheve's Jews were concentrated in one area of Oyber-Visheve. My family, however, lived outside the main Jewish neighborhood, together with other Jews who were spread out among the German families of Oyber-Visheve. In fact, our home was the very last Jewish lot, and only German families lived in the streets beyond our house.

My father usually *davened* in a small *shtiebel* in our neighborhood. It was located only minutes from our house and served three or four *minyanim* of Yidden. However, for *yomim tovim* and special occasions, we would cross the *hultzene brik,* the wooden bridge, near our house and walk a kilometer and a half (about a half hour) to the *Internat,* the *shul* where Reb Menachem Mendel Hager *davened.*

In truth, there were two large *shuls* in Oyber-Visheve. The first was known as the Groise Shul. It was located in the center of town, on the corner of Main Street and the Yiddishe Gas, about twenty-five yards away from the other *kehillah* buildings. Eight or ten majestic steps led to the women's entrance on Main Street. The men's entrance was on the Yiddishe Gas. There was a large yard in front of the men's entrance with a well in the center. A wooden barrel sat beside the well and it was regularly refilled so that the men could wash their hands. The water was spilled onto the ground, where a narrow ditch led the water away.

This *shul* had no *mezuzah* or *seforim* and served solely as a *bais haknesses.* It was an imposing structure with beautiful pictures painted on the ceiling and walls. Reb Berish Horowitz the Shochet was the *chazan,* and he typically led the *tefillos* for 300 or 400 people.

Behind the Groise Shul was another structure where people learned and where regular *minyanim* were held for those who chose not to *daven* with the *chazan* in the Groise Shul.

The town's second-largest *shul* was the *Internat*, where my father sometimes *davened* and where his family had a seat that had been passed down for several generations. The *Internat* was located on Main Street, about 100 or 150 yards uptown of the Groise Shul. I think its name implied that it was a central place that served multiple functions.

The *Internat* sat on the same property as the Rav's house. A large yard bordered the street, and like the yard in front of the Groise Shul, there was a well and wooden barrel in the center. The Rav's residence was on one side, and the *Internat* was just beyond the yard in the opposite direction. It was a large, three-story structure that housed both the Rav's *shul*, as well as Visheve's *yeshiva*, Beis Yisrael. The Vishever Rav also served as the Rosh Yeshiva of Beis Yisrael, and in fact, it was the largest *yeshiva* in all of Marmorosh, with 300-400 boys in its dormitory.

As the *yeshiva* grew, more space was required in the study halls and dormitory. Therefore, in 1934 or '35, the Sheiris Menachem left for the United States to collect funds to expand the *shul* and *yeshiva*. I was a young child at the time, about five or six years old. I distinctly recall how the townspeople escorted him with song and music. After he returned, he began rebuilding the *Internat* and also added a kitchen in the basement. Until then, the *bachurim* would eat *teig* by the local residents, as was the custom in many European towns. The *bachurim* were assigned specific days (or "*teig*") by local families, who could not always afford to provide them with nourishing meals. Once the *yeshiva* had its own kitchen, the boys ate their meals in the *yeshiva's* basement and no longer had to rely on the goodwill of local residents.

The first floor of the *Internat* was the *beis medrash*, which had 500 or 600 seats after it was expanded. A large wooden *aron kodesh* stood against the wall, with two beautifully carved eagles that sat facing each other at the top. The women's section was behind the opposite wall. At all hours, *chassidim* could be found learning inside the *beis medrash,* and on Shabbos and other special occasions, the Rav *fiered tisch* there. On *yomim tovim,* more townspeople came, as well as *chassidim* from neighboring Mittel-Visheve. They would bring their own chairs, and the *shul* would fill with some 2,000 or 2,500 congregants.

The second floor of the *Internat* contained the study rooms for the *bachurim* of the *yeshiva.* The third floor served as their dormitory. Beneath the *shul* was a finished basement with a dining room and kitchen for the *yeshiva* students.

Though the kitchen and expanded dormitory were of great benefit to the *yeshiva,* the rebuilding project was still not completed when the Hungarians took control of the region in 1940. Sadly, after the Jewish people were evacuated in 1944, they turned the building into their headquarters, using the first floor, the *shul,* as a stable for their horses, and the upper floor, the dormitory, for their soldiers.

There was a beautiful fruit garden in the yard behind the *Internat,* and it was filled with different fruit trees. A gazebo stood in the center of the garden, and during the summer, I would peek in with other children to observe the Rav learning there.

As the Rav of Visheve, the Sheiris Menachem was not only the leader of the local Vizhnitz community, but of the entire area. [3] On Shabbos Shuva and Shabbos HaGadol, *davening* started extra early in the *Internat* and in the other *shtieblach* in Visheve. Before *leining,* everyone would walk over to the Groise Shul, where Reb Mendel would deliver his Shabbos Shuva or Shabbos HaGadol *drasha.* The *shul* would fill with over 1,000 people, most of whom remained standing, as there were not enough seats. Afterwards, the Rav and other townspeople

---

3   It is worth mentioning that my father was on the committee that brought Reb Menachem Mendel to Visheve. The previous Rav, Rav Eliezer Dovid Greenwald, the Keren L'Dovid, served as the Rav of Visheve from 1912 until 1921, when he became Rav in Satmar. My father was a *talmid* of the Keren L'Dovid from an early age.

would return to finish *davening* in their own *shuls*.

As Vishever Rav, Reb Mendel also earned the respect of the non-Jewish residents of our town. Each year, on the tenth of May, the entire country celebrated Romania's Independence Day. All the boys wore formal outfits and the girls wore black berets, white blouses, and navy skirts. The local schools brought all their students to the main plaza in the center of town, where they gathered with the town's citizens. There, everyone heard speeches from the mayor and other town officials. Interestingly enough, Reb Mendel Hager was among those honored to address the crowd.

Though we lived outside of the Jewish neighborhood, we were on good terms with our neighbors, Zipser Germans, who had been living in the region for centuries. They spoke a distinctive dialect, Outzäpsersch (or Old Zipserish), which a number of Jews, including Uncle Baruch, learned to speak fluently. A small number of Hungarians also lived in our town.

While the Marmorosh region, with its tall mountains and flowing rivers, is very beautiful, it is also a place of long, harsh winters. Additionally, the mountainous terrain and short summers are not conducive to growing a large variety of vegetation. As a result, there were few wealthy people in the Visheves, and most families lived simple, unsophisticated lives, making do with basic needs.

Most of Visheve's streets were made out of gravel, and our only means of transportation were horses and wagons. From mid-October to April, when the ground was covered with snow, the wagons were replaced with large sleds. Each April when the snow melted, the streets would become terribly muddy, and we had to take off our shoes when we arrived home to avoid bringing the muck and grime into our house.

The homes in Visheve had no running water so we used water from the well. For many years, we had no electricity either. At some point, a turbine was installed next to the *eizene brik*, or steel bridge, which spanned the Vaser River, a right tributary of the Vişeu River. While the *hultzene brik* was located right near our house, this steel bridge was about fifteen or twenty minutes away by foot, in the center of town. A short canal led away some water from the river to power the turbine, generating electricity for our town.

Of course, even with our "modern" turbine, life in Visheve remained very primitive. We still had no electrical outlets or appliances, only one or two light bulbs, which were installed only in a few select homes in the 1930's. Later, after the territory of Northern Transylvania (including all of Maramures) was reassigned to Hungary in September 1940, electricity was installed in more homes, including ours.

I distinctly remember when wires were first pulled to our home and we too got our first light bulb. The period stands out in my mind because that same winter, in January of 1941, the Vishever Rav was *niftar*. My maternal grandfather, Reb Shmiel Chaim Rosenfeld, came from Vilchovitz together with the Rav's brother, the Vilchovitzer Rav, for the *levaya*.

I only saw my maternal grandfather three or four times in my life, so his visit to Visheve was a cause of much celebration in our home. He stayed with us for Shabbos, and on Friday night, we children remained seated at the Shabbos table until late, unwilling to part from our *Zeide* and go to sleep. Eventually, my father chased us all into bed, but I made sure to awake extra early on Shabbos morning to be able to spend time with my *Zeide* again.

When I came out of bed, I was surprised to find my grandfather sitting with a *sefer* in the exact spot that I had seen him the previous night. "*Tatte, Der Zeide is nisht geshlufen?*" I asked. ("Did Grandfather not sleep?")

My father repeated my question to the *Zeide* with a smile. "*Bei aza sheine licht, vi ken men shlufen?*" my grandfather replied. ("By such a beautiful light, how can one sleep?") Indeed, it was still a novelty at the

time to own a light bulb, which could burn all night and allow someone to learn for hours after dark.

Incidentally, residents were not charged for electricity according
to how much they used it, but rather according to the wattage of their
light bulbs. An inspector would visit each home periodically to check
the light bulbs, which were usually about twenty-five or fifty watts.
Each home was then charged accordingly. (I remember the wife of
my private *melamed* stalling the inspector outside so that her husband
could quickly change the bulb in their kitchen to one that had fewer
watts, thus lowering the cost of their electricity…)

In the Visheves, telephones were even rarer than light bulbs. Only
two or three private people owned a telephone. The main telephone for
our town was located inside the post office. If someone wanted to make
a phone call, he had to write a postcard one or two weeks in advance to
let the person know to wait in the post office at a specific day and time
for the phone call. In reality, such calls were rarely made and I don't
recall my family ever using this service.

Radios were similarly quite rare, and anyone who had an antenna
outside had to pay a special fee. The few Jews who owned a radio were
generally considered modern people, who were more sophisticated
and worldly than most of the town's Jews.

Most Jews in Visheve supported their families by working as
melamdim, skilled tradesmen, or store owners. Most of the Germans,
on the other hand, either raised honeybees or worked as loggers. In
fact, Vişeu de Sus was part of a forestry railway system that extended
deep into the Vaser river valley. Lumber produced from the forests in
our region played an important role in the local economy. During the
summer, many of our neighbors spent weeks at a time in the mountains chopping wood. The wood was then trimmed into nice, round
logs and tied together to form large platforms. The platforms would be
placed onto the river and guided downstream by a logger who stood
on the platform with a large, wooden paddle.

Typically, the river near our home was only about two or three feet deep and ten yards wide. However, there was a dam upstream that the loggers would open to flood the river when they had to send down their log platforms. Many times, the water's strong current misdirected the logs, and they tore down the *hultzene brik*. When this happened, a temporary footbridge would be erected using boards as the floor and ropes on the sides. This greatly inconvenienced the local residents, who had to walk to the *eizene brik* if they wanted to cross the river with their horses and wagons filled with wares or supplies. This situation would last for a week or two, until repairs could be completed on the *hultzene brik*.

Eventually, the *hultzene brik* was rebuilt. The new wooden bridge had supports only at the two ends and none in the center of the river and was also taller than the old one. These improvements benefited the families of our neighborhood tremendously since we were no longer left stranded without proper access to the other side of the river. Additionally, since the new bridge was a covered bridge, residents were able to take shelter there during unexpected rainfalls. This was particularly helpful to farmers who sold hay in large, tall wagons, as they were able to lead their horses onto the bridge and keep their hay dry.

Near the logging business was an ice cutting industry. Since there was no refrigeration in the area, ice was essential to the homes and businesses to keep the food fresh. Blocks of ice, one cubic foot each, were cut out of the frozen lake and sold to stores and families. After a few days, the lake froze over again and new blocks of ice could be harvested.

Another source of income in our region was the ski resort set among the mountains near our home. We children watched in fascination as elegantly dressed people poured into town, arriving on first-class trains from Budapest. They passed our neighborhood as they headed towards the nearby resort, where they spent their vacations skiing on the mountains.

In the summertime, another natural wonder attracted vacationers to the region: seven natural springs with different kinds of mineral waters. Located about two or three kilometers from our house, the place was called Valea Vinului and the mineral water springs were called *borcut*. People would drink the springs' pure, refreshing water and take therapeutic baths in the boiling sulfur. Sometimes, my father would rent a cabin for our family near the springs. He would take the boys to bathe in the water and my mother would take the girls.

All these businesses and vacation spots were mostly operated by the local Germans. The Romanians of our region led a lifestyle that was vastly different from the Jews and the Germans. They were farmers who lived off the land in the surrounding mountains. They built their own log cabins and grew vegetables, including corn, which they crushed into flour. They also had many fruit trees and farm animals. They wore unusual clothes that were made out of the wool that was shorn from their sheep. Their shoes were pointy in the front and fashioned out of paper-thin rubber. The rubber was about 9x12 inches, with holes cut into them. Leather strings were used to sew the top and bottom together through the holes and to tie the shoe around the ankle and leg. They typically wrapped some *shmattes* around their legs and then tied the strings over that.

My father owned a general store, so we interacted regularly with all our neighbors. This store had been opened by his parents, on whose property our home was built. Uncle Baruch later opened an even larger general store, which was located on the main Jewish street uptown, across the street from the big *shul*.

The Jews and Germans in our town came to our store to purchase flour, fruit, chocolate, kerosene, and other necessities. The Romanians would visit periodically, bartering vegetables, potatoes, eggs, corn flour, and even chickens, for oil, kerosene, and other items. In the summer, they'd also bring blueberries, strawberries, hazelnuts, and walnuts that my father then sold to our customers.

The most commonly used flour in the Visheves was corn flour, which was ground in the mills in our town. The fine flour that my father offered our customers was purchased from neighboring regions. This was the flour my mother used for bread and *challos.*

In addition to all the regular items he stocked, my father often offered specific items that his customers needed. For example, the main staples of the Romanian farmers during the winter were potatoes and cabbage. Each winter, the snow would fall in October, right after Succos, and stay on the ground until early spring. During this time, carrots, parsley, onions, and other vegetables were not available. Instead, the Romanians purchased pounds of cabbage and stored them in large barrels that contained 20 or 30 kilos of cabbage each. My father would purchase a railroad car load of this cabbage to have enough to supply the local farmers.

Another specialty item was *bryndza,* the cheese my father made for the loggers. The loggers would stay up in the mountains for weeks at a time and needed nutritious foods that were easy to prepare. Therefore, during the logging season, they purchased a lot of corn flour and *bryndza.* The *bryndza* was made of seventy-five percent sheep cheese, a very fat cheese with a strong odor, and twenty-five percent cow cheese, which was needed to hold the sheep cheese together. We used a large hand grinder to grind the cheeses together. Then, we filled barrels of ten to fifteen kilos of *bryndza* and sent them up to the loggers with kerosene and other necessities. Sometimes, one of the workers came to pick everything up. Then, about once or twice a month, the foreman would come into the store and pay for the workers' supplies.

Like all children, the children in Visheve attended school regularly. The day at public school was typically four hours long, usually from eight until twelve, although sometimes there were two alternating shifts, with the second group of children attending class from twelve until four. There, the teachers and students spoke Romanian and Hungarian.

The Jewish children had a longer school day, since they attended *cheder* too. The local Talmud Torah, which was supported by the *kehillah* tax, was considered to provide somewhat of an inferior education. Only the children of poor families attended this *cheder*. The children of more *balabatishe* families studied with private teachers. These teachers didn't teach each student individually, rather they created their own classes, which they taught in their homes. However, because their livelihood depended on their reputation as an educator, they were more motivated to provide a higher level of education so that they would continue attracting students.

There were a number of private teachers in our town, some who taught *kriah,* others Chumash, and several Gemara. Each *rebbe* catered to a specific age range and academic level. Before Rosh Chodesh Elul, and then again around Rosh Chodesh Nissan, the *melamdim* would go from father to father, trying to recruit ten to fifteen students for their class for the coming *z'man.* Parents would ask, "Whom do you have?" and the *rebbe* would begin listing his clientele. "Shlomo Tessler's two sons will be learning with me," he would say, for example. In this way, he hoped to attract more students and fill up his class.

As *cheder* students, we started our day very early. At six in the morning, we had to be at the *rebbe's* house. Then we'd run home for breakfast and rush back out to be on time at public school. After twelve o'clock, we returned home for lunch and then went back to *cheder.* We had a short break for supper and then continued learning until nine. Thus, for us Jewish boys, it was a very long school day, from early in the morning until after dark. Our yearly breaks only came from Rosh Chodesh Nissan until after Pesach, and from before Tishrei until after Sukkos.

Of course, sending all his boys to private *rebbes* cost a pretty penny, but my father spared no cost when it came to our Jewish education. Moreover, every Rosh Chodesh, my father would send Rosh Chodesh *gelt* to our *rebbes.* This monthly tip was carefully wrapped in a piece of paper and given to each child to deliver to his *rebbe.*

In order to make sure that we were doing well in our studies, he would stop by the *rebbe's* house every week or two to check up on us. He was very diplomatic about his visits and didn't make us feel like he was intruding on our day. Instead, he would drop by with an apple, for example, and say, "*Di Mamme hut geshikt an appel.*" Other times he would bring an egg or a piece of cake. Since we knew his appearance meant that there would be a treat for us, we were happy to see him. He would motion for the *rebbe* to keep teaching and remain for several minutes to watch our progress.

In addition to these visits to our class, my father would spend each Friday night and Shabbos day reviewing with all of us the material that we had covered that week. It was very clear to us boys that our father considered our Jewish education a priority, and we tried our best to make him proud.

Our *rebbes* did not only teach Chumash and Gemara but also Yiddish writing. This was a subject that posed some challenges for me, since I am a lefty by nature but was forced to write with my right hand. Whenever the *rebbe* glanced in another direction, I switched hands, but then he would take my quill and stab me on the side of my left hand with its sharp tip so that I wouldn't write with that hand. In fact, I still have marks from all those stabbings during writing class. (Today I write with my right hand, as I was forced to do in school, but when I cut with a knife or do other things, I use my left hand, which is really my dominant hand.)

While the girls in our town did not attend *cheder*, some families hired private teachers to teach them at home. This was not the standard in every home, since many women in our town were uneducated and did not know how to read. In fact, in the *veiber shul*, there would be one woman who said the *tefillos* out loud while the other women listened. However, my parents were both considered highly educated, and neighbors would bring letters to my mother for her to read to them. As such, my parents made it a priority to educate their daughters too, and I vaguely remember a teacher coming to teach Goldy and

Frady to read *Ivrah.*

Attending public school was not always easy for Jewish children. Though teachers warned students not to fight, somehow there were always skirmishes between Romanian, German, or Hungarian students and the Jewish children. There were soccer teams in our school, and during games, whether we were playing or watching from the sidelines, fights sometimes broke out. Non-Jewish students liked to start up with the younger Jewish children, and I remember being attacked when I was in the younger grades. When our older brothers would hear our cries, they would come running to rescue us from the bullies.

Additionally, we endured a difficult period in 1936 or '37, after Romanian officials decided that there would be school on Shabbos too. This decision was motivated purely by anti-Semitism, since school on Saturday was really not the norm.

I was a little boy then, six or seven years old, and I had to bring my writing material with me to school. We couldn't simply stay home, since parents were fined for truancy if their children were absent without a good reason. In fact, the local officials could come to the home and remove pillows or valuables, for which the parents then had to barter to get back.

I remember that before we left to school on Shabbos my father was very anxious. He told us to *daven* quickly, since we would be unable to attend *shul.* Then he told us to leave our pencils at home. "If they give you another pencil to write with, break off the point," he instructed.

Our school had a canteen, which sold pencils and school supplies, among other things. Whenever students were missing supplies, the teacher would tell them to take a new one from the canteen, and the school would then charge the parents for the cost. Therefore, my father knew that if we didn't take our supplies, we would receive new ones from the canteen, for which he would later have to pay. He was ready to cover that expense, but he wanted to make sure we still would not write. Moreover, since he knew it would be difficult for us to face our teachers, he checked our pockets before we left to make sure that we were not sneaking pencils to school.

This difficult situation went on for a few weeks or months. Eventually, the Jewish parents were able to pay off the official in charge and the new regulation magically disappeared. After all, in Romania, getting what you wanted was simply a matter of finding the right price.

Chapter Two:
Of Hearth and Home

My parents, Shlomo and Esther Tessler, were strict but fair. We children knew to respect whatever they said, yet at the same time we felt cared for and loved.

My father was about six feet tall, and his imposing figure demanded respect. He was a great scholar who was very pious and meticulous in *mitzvos*. He also had a good business sense and traveled throughout the region to purchase goods for our store.

My mother was a tall, beautiful woman, with high cheekbones and an aristocratic air about her. She was very intelligent and held in high esteem by other women in our town. She was a commanding, energetic woman, who moved quickly and constantly as she cared for her large family.

My parents had nine children: Naftuli, the oldest, was born in November of 1926. He was the big brother whom I adored and followed around everywhere. Predictably, he didn't particularly appreciate having me tail him around constantly.

Baruch, the second son, was born in February 1928. I was born next in September of 1929. My Hebrew name is Menachem Dov, but I've always been known by its Yiddish form, Mendel Ber. Since I was only one and a half years younger than Baruch, we were very close and spent our days together, both in cheder and at home.

Next was my dear sister Goldie, the oldest daughter born in February of 1931. She was a beautiful girl, tall for her age, and my mother's right hand. We had a special bond, since we were so close in age, and I loved her very much.

Hershy was born in October of 1932. He was a very smart boy who learned exceptionally well. My father enjoyed reviewing his learning with him. Once my mother asked him, "Why are you bothering Hershy so much? Does he know his material or not?" My father replied, "He knows everything very well, but I want to see if he just knows to repeat it or if he really *understands* what he learned."

Frady (named after our Tessler grandmother) was born in February 1934 and Yida Meir in December of 1936. The two youngest children were Toba Gittel, born in April 1938, and little Moshe Yitzchok, born in May of 1940.

As I grew older, I spent many hours in *cheder*, so I don't have many memories of the younger children. I do remember, though, that Toby had very curly hair and screamed loudly each time my mother combed it out. I also recall that she and Moishy spent all their time together, often running across the street to our neighbor's home. The neighbors earned their livelihood by sewing small powder puffs that women used to apply makeup. When the two returned home, their pockets were always filled with little pieces of this soft fabric.

We lived on a property that had once belonged to our Tessler grandparents. Their old house still stood on the lot, and in fact, Uncle Baruch had lived there with them until he moved uptown with his growing family to open his own store.

Next to that house was a large structure that had a room in the front and a large stable for cows in the back. We didn't use that stable, and after my grandmother's passing in 1933, my grandfather slept in that room together with Baruch and me. At times, such as when my father had to serve in the army, my grandfather stayed with Uncle Baruch, but whenever he lived with us, it was our job to care for him.

I remember once when Uncle Baruch visited and he saw some crumbs on our grandfather's beard. "What will people say if you don't keep *Der Zeide* clean?" he admonished us. He then gave us two *lei* to motivate us to keep looking after our *Zeide* properly.

This large structure in which my grandfather slept was later used by Romanian soldiers. They came to our town in the late 30's and assigned groups of soldiers to people's homes. It served their purposes well, and the soldiers even put horses in the stable and cannons in the yard.

The store stood between my grandparents' old house and our house. Behind the store, was a large structure with three sections. One was a big warehouse for the store; the second was filled with shelves and served as a pantry for storing preserved foods, smoked meats, and other items; and the third was a barn for geese that my mother raised each year for Pesach *schmaltz*. Under the first section, the store warehouse, we also had our ice pit. A wooden ladder led straight down into a small, cold cellar where we stored food that had to be kept cold. At the top of the structure, a large loft stretched above all three sections and was used to store hay for our cows. We also stored apples there after the summer, where they stayed fresh for a long time.

My family's home was built on the other side of the store and consisted of two large rooms. The front room served as a dining room and master bedroom. On one side, there was a big dining room table, large enough for the entire family and even some guests to eat together, and it was surrounded by upholstered dining room chairs. On the other side of that room were two beds, both along the same wall, as was the custom then in our community, where my parents slept with the youngest children. On the opposite wall was a large couch, where three or four children slept. There was also a large closet where clothing was stored.

The back room had the kitchen on one side, with the oven and stove attached to the wall and a kitchen table with two benches, where the family ate during the week. On the other side of the room stood a large utility table that could be converted into a wide bed. We opened it up each night and four children would sleep there.

At the front entrance of our house we had a large porch that served as another room during the summer. When the weather turned nice, we put a big table on the porch and ate there on Shabbos morning and afternoon. Or, when we made a *bris,* we would serve the poor people on the porch.

Behind the house stood our year-round *sukkah* room, which also had a *shlock,* a roof that we could open with pulleys. This *sukkah* room was separated from our home by the chicken coop that stood between the two structures. This room served multiple purposes, functioning both as a summer kitchen and as an extra bedroom for guests. A metal stove in the *sukkah* room was used to cook during the summer and to heat the room on Sukkos.

Near the *sukkah* room we had an outhouse as well as our family's garden. There were some apple trees and plum trees and patches of carrots, scallions, radishes, parsley, potatoes, and string beans. We planted the vegetables after Pesach, and once they ripened, we picked whatever we needed each day.

My mother was a busy woman with her hands full, caring for her large family, keeping the house clean, cooking our meals from scratch, and supervising the maids. She had one or two Romanian maids to help her, and these young women slept in my grandfather's room when he was not there. They helped my mother by milking the one or two cows we always had, feeding the chickens, bringing in wood, washing the floors, and cleaning the house. The one thing they never helped my mother with was cutting up and cooking our food, since my parents wanted to make sure the food met their high standards of *kashrus.* Incidentally, my father also never made *brochos* in front of the maids and would wait for them to go to the other room.

At least clothing the children was somewhat easier than it is today. Twice each year, before the winter and after Pesach, a seamstress would come to our house and measure everyone for shirts, pants, and underwear. Everything was custom made and taken care of without too much hassle.

While obtaining clothes was relatively easy, washing them was no simple matter. We had a round wooden laundry barrel that was called a *zeichtl*. It was about three feet in diameter and stood on three claw feet. There was a hole on the bottom, and a special, long pole was fitted into the hole to plug it before the barrel was filled with water.

On Wednesdays, my mother would put the pole in place and begin stacking clothes inside the barrel. She would alternate between clothes and some powdered soap, putting layer upon layer inside. When the barrel was full, she spread a sheet on top, added wooden ashes, and then covered the ashes with another sheet. The sheets kept the ashes from falling between the clothes, and the ashes caused a chemical reaction that helped with the cleaning process. Though it may seem counterintuitive to use ashes to clean clothes, this was a technique used by all the housewives in the region. Finally, once the ashes were inside, my mother filled the barrel with hot water and left the clothes to soak overnight.

On Thursdays, our maid would pull out the long pole to allow the water to drain from the bottom of the barrel. Then, she would take small stacks of clothes at a time in a basin to the river. The river was only two houses from our home, and several flat rocks were situated right beside it. The maids and housewives from the neighborhood spread the clothes on these rocks and rubbed them with a *pranik*. This was a piece of wood, about eighteen inches long and half-an-inch thick, which had a wide handle attached to it. It was used to bang on the clothes and rub the stains until the laundry was ready to be rinsed in the river. Of course, this was even harder in the winter, when there was a foot of ice on the river's surface, and it had to be chopped away before the clothes could be rinsed.

When the pile of clothes was clean, the maid returned to bring the next stack to rub and rinse by the river. She made several such trips until all the clothes had been removed from the barrel.

Before *yomim tovim* and other busy times, when tablecloths, towels, and bed spreads were also washed, my mother would have two maids rubbing and rinsing the laundry. Typically, though, only one maid helped with this work.

Between Shabbos preparations and laundry, Thursday was always a hectic day. Not only were the clothes washed, but they also had to be ironed with my mother's coal iron. As such, each Thursday evening, we were served the same, simple supper. My mother would put up a large pot of pinto beans. Some of them were mashed and combined with sautéed onions for a filling side dish. The rest were used to make a thick soup that we called *chipkelech mitt bundlech. Chipkelech* are square noodles, and together with the beans, they were the main ingredients of this quick and easy soup, which we ate with bread.

Thus, my mother managed to provide her family with a filling meal while still keeping up with her work. Indeed, my mother was an exceptional housekeeper and cook. She kept the house in order and prepared simple but scrumptious dishes for our family. She prepared mostly dairy and vegetables for us during the week, with the exception of one meat dinner mid-week, usually of smoked meat, which we made in the winter from geese. Additional meat dishes and other treats were reserved for Shabbos.

Somehow, my mother managed to cook all our delicious meals and tasty desserts in our primitive kitchen. We didn't have a refrigerator or sink of course. We kept food cold in the ice pit and collected water from a well next to our house.

The stove top in our kitchen was somewhat similar to gas stoves in homes today. It measured two feet wide and about three feet deep. There were two holes, about a foot in diameter, and they were covered with cast iron plates. Above these were a series of about four cast iron rings, each one about an inch larger in diameter than the one before it. When my mother wanted to use a small pot, she removed only one ring to allow a small fire to emerge through the stovetop. For a bigger pot, she also removed the second ring. Thus, the rings allowed her to adjust the flame according to the size of the pot.

The brick oven beneath the stove was larger, about four or five feet wide and six feet deep. Each Thursday my mother would use it to bake bread for the coming week, and on Friday, she baked *challos* and two or three cakes for Shabbos.

Operating an old-fashioned brick oven was no simple matter and required much preparation. Each summer my father would buy one wagonload of soft wood and two wagonloads of hard wood. Local workmen would come to our house to chop up the wood in our yard. They would place a log on a platform between them and hold a large saw that had a handle that was about a foot tall on each side. They would move the saw back and forth together, back and forth between them, until a one-foot piece would fall off the log. They would do this again and again until the entire log was cut up. Later, the pieces of wood were cut up even more, into little squares or rectangles, about two inches wide.

Cutting up a wagonload of wood would take the workmen two full days. When they were done, the men would stack the wood outside, against the side wall of the house. Usually, the soft and hard wood were purchased and cut up at different times, and each type of wood would be stacked separately.

Whenever my mother wanted to bake, she would first light *shpin-dlech*, or tinder, small pieces of paper and thin twigs that were needed to start a fire. Once there were flames, pieces of soft wood kindling were added to allow the fire to grow. They would be crisscrossed, one on top of the other, so that the wood wouldn't choke the fire but allow it to burn through the stack. Then, once the fire was strong, she added the hard wood for durability, as this allowed the fire to last a long time. Once the fire was going strong and preheating the oven, my mother would begin mixing ingredients in a wooden bowl that had been formed out of a hollowed tree trunk. She had two or three of these bowls, and they were large enough to hold ten to fifteen kilos (more than twenty pounds) of flour.

When the oven was hot and the food was ready to bake, she used a shovel to bring all the ashes and burning embers to the front. She would then put in the *challos* or cake using a flat, round kitchen utensil with an extended arm (similar to what is used in a matzah bakery). She added wood as needed and turned the baked goods occasionally until the challos, cake or bread were done.

There was also a *pripitchik*, or hearth, that extended from the oven and was about two feet high and three feet wide. This space was like a ledge that was open on the inside and provided a warm place for us young children to curl up. It was the warmest place in the house.

Most of the people in our town did not have ovens. In fact, every *Erev Shabbos*, the alarm from the town's *mikvah* sounded three times. The first time it reminded the townspeople to bring their *cholent* to the baker's large oven, where it was kept warm until the following day, when they would pick it up at around noon. (There was an *eiruv* in town.) Fifteen minutes later it rang again to remind those that had stores to close up their shops. Finally, the last alarm sounded to let families know that it was time to light the Shabbos candles.

In our house, we did not send the *cholent* to the baker, because my parents didn't *mish* with anyone else. Just like we didn't eat the bakery bread sold in our store or pastries from the local Jewish baker, we also didn't put our *cholent* pot in the baker's oven. So, when the first alarm sounded, we placed the *cholent* in our own oven and sealed it. The burning embers kept it warm until we removed it on Shabbos afternoon.

There were two bakeries in our town. One sold rolls and bread, and the other made *rugelech* and cakes. Not seven-layer cakes or other fancy pastries, of course, but simple apple or honey cakes, *kokosh* cake, and *torts* (round sponge or nut cakes). My father, who was very meticulous in matters of *kashrus*, only ate food prepared by my mother in our home. He never purchased any bakery products for us (though occasionally we children managed to get our hands on them). We didn't feel deprived, though, because my mother baked her own delicious cakes. She made *kokosh* cake for *simchos* and special occasions, and large pans of honey and sponge cakes regularly for Shabbos. She also made a delicious apple cake, which had a layer of apples on the bottom and a cake batter that was poured over it.

In fact, not only did we enjoy my mother's culinary creations, but she baked for some of our German customers too! It seems that other women in our town knew that she was quite proficient in the kitchen. When they came to the store before the holidays to purchase ingredients, some of them asked my mother to bake cakes for their families. As a courtesy for select, frequent customers, my mother would take the flour and other ingredients they had purchased and prepare one of her simple but delicious cakes. (Incidentally, while my sisters loved licking the batter off the mixing bowls after my mother baked, she never allowed them to lick off batter from cakes she made for our non-Jewish customers. Since the ingredients had already been purchased, she considered it food that belonged to a non-Jew and did not want my sisters to eat from it.)

In addition to the fresh *challos* and cakes that my mother prepared for Shabbos, she also made fish, chicken, soup, potato *kugel*, cornmeal *kugel, tzimmes* (sweetened carrots), and compote.

On a special Shabbos, there would be some additional delicacies, such as *lukshen kugel*, which was made with noodles, nuts, fat, and spices. Another special *kugel* was called *gebleterte kugel*. It was a round *kugel*, about the size of a pie. My mother would roll out a dough and cut it into large circles. Then she prepared a mixture that included ground nuts, oil, and honey. Afterwards, she layered the dough and the mixture, one on top of the other.

This *gebleterte kugel* took a long time to prepare and was reserved for very special occasions. In fact, I remember my mother making this *kugel* when the Vilchovitzer Rav came with my grandfather to Visheve after the *petirah* of the Vishever Rav. Since my brother's Bar Mitzvah was only a few weeks later, my grandfather asked the Vilchovitzer Rav if Baruch could say his *pshetel* at the *tisch*. The Rav did not usually allow *chassidim* to share *divrei Torah* during the *tisch*, but he agreed to my grandfather's request. In honor of the occasion, my mother prepared a couple of cakes and a *gebleterte kugel*.

It is worth mentioning an incident that occurred during that *tisch*. As soon as Baruch started saying his *pshetel*, he was interrupted by the Lerdene *shochet*, a man who had earned the honor of starting the crowd's singing during *darashos* at Bar Mitzvas, *chasunos*, and other occasions.

"Can the Rav please allow Baruch to finish the *pshetel* that he practiced?" my grandfather asked.

The Rav, later known as the Imrei Chaim of Vizhnitz, replied, "On my *chazakah*, that nobody talk during the *tisch*, I could be *mevater*, but his *chazakah*, to start the singing, I cannot take away. But I promise you that he will continue his *pshetel* at his *chasunah*."

In the difficult years that followed, my father and brother considered this statement as a *brachah* from the Rebbe for Baruch's survival.

Since so much effort went into preparing the food each Shabbos, we truly cherished the peace and serenity that Shabbos brought. Once my mother *tzind lecht*, a calm and quiet enveloped our home. The little ones were fed before the *z'man*, and after the men and boys left for *shul*, no one ate anything until after Kiddush.

When my father came home, he sat down at the head of the table. Naftuli sat to his right, followed by Baruch and then me. Goldie sat to his left, and she was followed by the girls and young children. My mother sat at the other end of the table, opposite my father. When guests came, Naftuli moved down, as did Baruch and I. I wasn't very happy when this happened, since this put me at the very end of the table, away from my father.

When each course was served, no one touched the food right away. We waited for my father to start eating and only then did we do the same.

During the morning *seudah*, we prepared a special paste called *p'tcha*. It was made of calf feet, garlic, and mashed egg yolk. We dunked pieces of challah into this mixture, and after they were completely coated, everyone received a piece. It was quite delicious, a special Shabbos treat that we eagerly anticipated.

Somehow, my mother had the special ability to stretch the food to satisfy not only her own large family but also any guests who showed up on our doorstep. In fact, this happened quite regularly, since there were always several *meshulachim* in *shul*. These collectors would sleep in the *hachnosas orchim* rooms in our town, and on Friday night, the *gabbai* assigned each one to eat with a different family for Shabbos.

My father was considered one of the *balabatishe yidden* of the town and he always took home one of the *meshulachim* to eat with our family. One regular guest was a fellow whom everyone called Reb Meir Biztug. He had earned this nickname because he worked as a tailor, and whenever people asked when their clothing would be ready, he said, "*Biz tug*." (Lit. "until day," or by the next morning.) Reb Meir always insisted on going to our house since my mother treated all the guests very nicely. In fact, he would refer to her as "Reb Esther."

Another regular guest was Vaader Yid, who came from the village of Vaad. No one wanted to take him home because he ate huge amounts of food; nonetheless, my parents often hosted him. Whenever he came to Visheve, he would go from house to house on Thursday collecting money. As such, my mother knew when to expect him and made sure to prepare enough food.

One time, the Vaader Yid was assigned to my father, and he arrived at our house after the Friday night *tefillos*. My mother had not seen him that Thursday and did not know he was in town. "Why didn't you tell me you're here?" she asked him. She sent one of the children to our store next door to bring bakery bread. This was very unusual since we did not eat the kosher bakery bread that was sold in our store. Now, however, my mother wanted to make sure there would be enough for everyone. She also stretched the rest of the food, so that she would be able to serve Vaader Yid with her usual generous portions.

Vaader Yid ate with us again the following day on Shabbos morning, but in the afternoon, when my father wanted to wash for *shalash seudos*, he did not show up. My father liked to wait until everyone was at the table before washing, but after a few minutes, he went ahead and started the meal. When my father returned to *shul* for *Maariv*, he met his Shabbos guest. "Vaader Yid, why didn't you come for *shalash seudos*?" he asked him.

"Your wife gave me so much food," the man replied. "I had a stomachache!"

Indeed, this was our mother: selfless and capable, as she cared for her husband and children and all who crossed our threshold. Even in our simple, wooden, two-room home, she made us feel like rich children who had everything that we needed.

CHAPTER THREE:
HOLY DAYS AND HAPPY TIMES

I n our home and in our town, life revolved around the Jewish calendar. In addition to Shabbos, the highlight of our week, there were the many *yomim tovim* that we celebrated together, each one with its own tastes and traditions.

Rosh Hashana and Yom Kippur were serious days, during which we spent many hours in *shul*. On Rosh Hashana we *davened* in the *shul* next to our house, and a man named Lox came from the big *shul* to *daven Mussaf* and *lein*.

Each year on Erev Yom Kippur, at about two in the morning, Berish the Shochet would come to our house. Since we had a large yard, it was the perfect place for all the neighbors to gather and have Berish *shecht* their chickens. Of course, the men had to purchase a *shechitah* ticket in advance. They each gave Berish their ticket together with *trink gelt,* or a tip, for making the long walk to our side of town.

On Yom Kippur, we walked to the *Internat,* the Rav's big *shul* in town. My father bought one seat in *shul* for himself, two for us boys to share, and one in the women's section for my mother and Goldie. Seats were very expensive, and many townspeople could not afford seats. They came to *shul* carrying their own stools, since there was an *eiruv* in town. Quite often, men from Mittel-Visheve sat down in my seat, much to my annoyance. My father would not tell them to move away and I would have to wait until they left to get my seat back.

Before Sukkos, we didn't have to build a *sukkah* from scratch, since we had our *sukkah* room in the yard. The *s'chach* in the *sukkah,* though, had to be replaced, since it remained there from Sukkos to Sukkos. We would take off the old *s'chach* and carefully prepare new *s'chach* in honor of *yom tov.* Afterwards, we would break the wood from the old *s'chach* and put it aside to light the stove for Simchas Torah.

Another activity before Sukkos was creating our own *noi sukkah.* My brothers and sisters were all involved in this activity, and my mother knew that she couldn't count on us for too much help. We took glossy colored paper, which my father sold in his store before Sukkos, and used it to create stars, often with the help of my mother. We also made chains out of narrow strips of colored paper.

Uncle Baruch liked to puncture two soft boiled eggs each morning and suck out the contents. Before Sukkos, we took these empty egg shells and attached colored paper to them to create birds with colorful wings. We used our own version of glue: a paste made with flour and water.

Simchas Torah was a very exciting time in our home. After the *seudah* on the first night of Simchas Torah, most people went to the Rebbe's *tisch,* which lasted until two or three in the morning. After the *tisch,* the men had a *minhag* to go from house to house. In each home, they were served wine, *holuptches* or other *yom tov* delicacies. Since ours was the very last Jewish home in Visheve, it was already about seven in the morning by the time the group of men arrived at our house. I remember Naftula Lox, my father's friend, calling out to my mother, "Esther, *geb arois dus essen vus iz doo*." ("Serve the food that you have.") But my mother handed my father his *talis* and said, "Shlomo, *es iz tzeit tzi gein daven'en*." ("It is time to go pray.") Davening on Simchas Torah started promptly at seven o'clock, and by the time the men arrived at our house, it was usually too late to eat.

On the second morning of *yom tov,* there was always a festive *kid-*

dush in our home. My father was Chasan Bereishis in his *shul* and all the people would come to our house after *davening*. The crowd of men would fill our dining room and front porch, as they enjoyed my mother's delicious, home-made cakes and *holuptches*.

Another Simchas Torah treat were the beautiful *koilish challos* that my mother baked. These *challos* were decorated with unique braids and traditionally served in honor of Purim and Simchas Torah. While the Purim *koilish* was big enough to feed everyone, my mother gave each of us boys our own small *koilish challah* on Simchas Torah. They were baked fresh on *yom tov*, and the whole house was filled with a heavenly aroma.

Chanukah was another time of celebration in our home. We didn't *tzind* the *menorah* in the front, because we were afraid of non-Jews, who were celebrating their own holiday at the time. Instead, we placed the *menorah* at our side door, the one which led to the yard and faced our store.

My father used candles, not oil, for his *menorah*. On the first night of Chanukah, he lit the first candle himself. On the second night, he lit the first candle and then gave the *shamash* to my mother to light the next one. On each night, the *shamash* would be passed around, from my father to my mother to Tuli, to Baruch, to me, to Goldie, and so on. Each one of us lit one candle on the *menorah*.

Each year, before or after Chanukah, my mother became very busy with a special Pesach preparation. Although Pesach was still months away, she already had to start thinking about making the *schmaltz*, the fat she used instead of oil each Pesach. The *schmaltz* was not only for our family, but she also sent two-gallon barrels of *schmaltz* to her father and sisters in Czechoslovakia.

To start the process, we got ten geese that were kept in the barn in the warehouse behind the store. The geese were fed well to fatten them up. Finally, my mother would buy ten *shechitah* tickets for geese and summon Berish the Shochet to our house. After the geese were slaughtered, a crew of four or five neighborhood women would come to help my mother cut up and *kasher* the geese.

After all the fat was collected, it was dissolved over the fire. The Pesach grates had been put onto the stovetop in the morning, of course, so all the fat was *kosher l'Pesach*.

As the fat dissolved, the *grieven,* or geese cracklings, were carefully removed and taken to the *sukkah* room. There, on our second stovetop, which she could use for *chometz,* my mother made *toiken mitt grieven. Toiken* means cornflower and water and this thick paste was a staple in our area. Poor people ate this as a main meal together with milk almost every day. A meat version of this staple was made by mixing the paste with *grieven.* Thus, each year after my mother prepared the *schmaltz,* we ate *toiken mitt grieven* for supper for the next several days.

Of course, the work wasn't done yet. All the meat from the geese had to be dealt with too. After taking care of the *schmaltz,* my mother and the women would cut up the meat in quarters. Then, chopped garlic and spices like paprika and pepper would be rolled into the meat, which was then tied up with strings. The tied up meat would be taken to a nearby property where eight tenants lived in apartments around a large communal hallway. The smoke from all the apartments was fed into a large, specially-designed chimney in the hallway, where the neighborhood housewives brought meat to smoke. The meat was hung in a designated place inside the chimney and left there for two or three weeks.

After we picked up our smoked meat, my mother stored it in the pantry next to the warehouse. Before doing so, she also sent some of the meat to the women who had assisted her in making the *schmaltz,* as payment for their time.

The next memorable occasion in our home was Purim, when the entire town was filled with joyous festivities. Many people dressed up as a shoemaker, a rabbi, a chimney cleaner, or some other character. Oftentimes, three or four young fellows would go from house to house, or to some prearranged gathering places, and put on a performance together. One particular fellow, Bentzion Tabak, who was the Rav's personal assistant, known as the *hauz bachur*, would impersonate the Rav. He would perform his *shtick* in several places around town before finally arriving at the *yeshiva* at around one in the morning. There, the Rav would be in the midst of conducting a Purim *tisch* for the *yeshiva bachurim* and hundreds of townspeople. Bentzion Tabak would jump onto the table and repeat his performance, this time in front of the Rav and the gathered *chassidim,* much to the delight of the crowd. Money that was collected by Bentzion Tabak and other performers was all donated to Keren Bachurim, a special fund to help the town's *yeshiva* students pay for basic necessities.

Soon after Purim, we began making preparations for Pesach, my favorite *yom tov*. On Rosh Chodesh Nissan we moved into the *sukkah* room and began eating all our meals there. Before we could return to the house, my father would help each of us brush off our hands and remove our shoes. This allowed my mother to unpack all her Pesach dishes and begin preparing for the big *yom tov* without worrying about any food or crumbs finding their way inside.

Everyone in our family was involved in preparing for Pesach. One of the jobs for us boys was helping my father air out the *seforim*. We would lay the ends of several long boards on kitchen chairs that were put outside in the yard. Then, we spread all the *seforim* on these boards. We opened each one and kept an eye on them for several hours to make sure that pieces of *sheimos* would not fly away with the breeze. Afterwards, we would put the *seforim* back inside, leaving only those that would be put on the table on *yom tov*. We would take this assortment of *chumashim, siddurim, and mishnayos* that were needed for Pesach and replace their paper covers. These covers were carefully attached to each *sefer* since they remained on the *seforim* from one Pesach to the next.

Another job during the pre-Pesach cleaning was bringing down my sisters' trunks from the attic. As soon as each girl was born, a trunk was set aside for them, and we had separate ones for Goldie, Frady, and Toby. Their dowry was slowly being prepared, as towels, tablecloths, and linens were added periodically to the trunks. Every year before Pesach these trunks were opened up and all the contents were aired out.

A week before Pesach, my mother baked the last batch of *challos* and bread in her regular kitchen. Afterwards, a woman came to re-seal our brick oven with clay. During the year, this woman was called whenever the oven appeared cracked or did not heat up right away due to gaps that allowed heat to escape. However, my mother always made sure to call her after baking the last *chametz* items before Pesach.

The woman who resealed the oven was very short. We watched in wonder as she would pull a large burlap bag over her head, sticking her arms through holes that were made on the sides. Then she would climb into the oven, and using a small lantern for light, she would smooth a new layer of clay over the bricks.

Shortly before Pesach, we boys accompanied our father to the lo-cal *matzah* bakery, which occupied a prominent place in our lives. The bakery was located near our *cheder* and began producing *matzos* from Chanukah time. We enjoyed observing the hustle and bustle around the bakery and occasionally pilfering a piece of warm *matzah*.

My father would wait for a dry, sunny day to bring home our *mat-zos* for Pesach. We would take along a special basket to hold the *mat-zah,* usually close to thirty pounds in all. My father would take twenty pounds of regular *matzos* and another eight or ten pounds of *shevarim,* broken matzos, which were sold for half the price. Right before *yom tov*, he also purchased *Erev Pesach matzos* to use for the *sedarim*.

There would be no set price for the *matzah*. Each family was charged according to their means. This sliding fee scale ensured that all townspeople would be able to afford *matzos* for their families, re-gardless of their financial situation.

I remember marveling one year how the man at the *matzah* bakery greeted my father warmly and treated me and my brothers like kings. Only two weeks before, he had chased me away together with other *cheder* boys who tried to smuggle a piece of *matzah* from the bakery, but now that I was there with my father, I was treated like a prince. When my father prepared to pay, the man said, "This year the price is very high. We must charge a lot because there are many poor people in town."

There was a well across the street from our house, near the home of Elya the Melamed. There was a little structure built around the opening of the well. We opened a door and used a chain mounted on a wheel to bring up the water. During the year, a few non-Jewish neighbors sometimes used this well, but before Pesach, we put a lock on the door so that only the Jewish families who lived on the block would use it. This ensured that no non-Pesach'dige dishes or crumbs would fall into the water. Even with these precautions in place, the water in our household was carefully filtered with a heavy cheesecloth before it was used for cooking.

It is interesting to note that we ate *chometz* even on the morning of Erev Pesach, unlike today when it seems like some people keep Pesach for ten days or more. My mother made *moon kindel* and nut *kindel* for her *mishloach manos* each Purim, and she would put away some to serve Erev Pesach.

My father spread a tablecloth on the floor in the dining room, and we all sat on it when eating our *kindel*. My mother also served another food that we called *balmish*. This was made by mixing corn flour with all the leftover cheese, milk, butter, honey, and sugar, and cooking everything together on the stove in the *sukkah*. It was a tasty treat that we enjoyed each Erev Pesach.

After everyone finished eating, my father made sure that we dusted off all the crumbs from our clothes. Afterwards, we took baths and went to sleep. The first Pesach food that we ate was potatoes with *schmaltz* and *grieven*, which was served later that afternoon. My mother continued preparing fresh Pesach food as needed each day of *yom tov*. We enjoyed *latkes, chremzlech, keizlech*, and other foods that were made primarily with potatoes.

On Pesach, we did not eat *gebrokts* after the age of six. The younger kids ate *matzah* with *kavah*, our own version of coffee, which was made with warm milk and no water. They used special Pesach dishes that were set aside specifically for *gebrokts*. For the adults, the primary Pesach foods, like today, were eggs, potatoes, *matzah,* chicken, meat, and wine. We ate no fish on Pesach at all.

During Pesach, my father was very anxious about keeping the *matzah* separate and dry. In fact, we had three tablecloths spread on the table for the meals, instead of the two that we used on a typical Shabbos. On Shabbos we used two white tablecloths because my mother would take off the top one after the *seudah* and shake it off outside. The second tablecloth ensured that the table always remained covered in white, even when the top tablecloth was removed.

On Pesach, we ate the *matzah* on the topmost tablecloth. Afterwards, all the *matzah* was removed from the table and the tablecloth was rolled up towards the center, forming a runner down the middle of the table. We continued eating on the second tablecloth, which was left clean of crumbs, as no one touched *matzah* anymore. The third tablecloth on the bottom, like the one on Shabbos, served to keep the table covered the entire time.

After Pesach, there was additional work involved as we transitioned back to eating *chometz*. There were no grocery stores where we could go to stock up on *chometz* items. My mother had to replenish foods like pasta and *farfel* on her own and she spent about a week doing so.

My mother started this momentous task several days after *yom tov.* She would take out her *lukshen breit*, which was a flat piece of wood, about one inch thick. One side of the board was designated for *pareve* foods and the other for dairy. The board looked similar to the Shabbos *blechs* that come with a front piece to cover the stove knobs. At the far end of the *lukshen breit*, a few inches extended upwards so that if the board was flipped over to the other side, that section became the front piece that extended down. As my mother rolled out dough using a *valger holtz* (rolling pin) that was about three feet long, she pressed against this front piece to keep the board in place. Finally, after several long days of continuous work, my mother would once again have a generous supply of *farfel* and different types of *lukshen* to serve her family.

About a month after we had finally settled back into a routine, it was time to begin preparing for Shavuous. Before *yom tov,* we collected flowers and branches from our yard and placed them around our house. We also had the traditional *milchige seuda,* for which my mother prepared cheese cake and danishes. We ate these dairy treats after Kiddush and then, after waiting for a half hour, continued with the *fleishige yom tov* meal.

In addition to the holidays, there were other special occasions that stand out in my mind.

A *bris,* for example, was a cause for great celebration. The new mother would remain confined to her bed for two weeks, and the *haiban,* the midwife who helped deliver the baby, would take care of her. There was a special *kimmel zip,* or caraway soup, with *nokelech* (dumplings) that she prepared especially for *kimpeturins.* When one smelled this soup, it was a sign that a *kimpeturin* was in the house.

During the *vach-nacht,* the baby was placed in a cradle and covered with candies. All the children of the neighborhood would come in and surround the cradle. They would *lein krishma* and then chant, "*Vifil neigel is du oifen dach, azoi fil malachim zulen shtein oif di vach*— As many nails as there are on the roof, so many *malachim* should stand watch (over the baby)." Afterwards, each child was rewarded with one of the candies. A few friends of the father also came to have some cake and drink *l'chaim.* The *haiban* then prepared cakes, a big *koilish challah,* meats, and other foods, which were served to close family and friends after the *bris.*

Bar Mitzvos in those times weren't quite as grand an occasion as they are today. The Shabbos before my Bar Mitzvah, I was given *Maftir* in *shul,* as was the standard then. No boys *leined* in the Visheves, with the rare exception of a *chashuve* family's child, like the son of a *dayan* or *rav.* Besides, since in Vizhnitz the boys were *oleh* the Shabbos *before* their Bar Mitzvah, *leining* wasn't even an option.

After *Shachris,* my father's friends came home with us from *shul* and were treated to a *kiddush.* This was the entire Bar Mitzvah celebration. Then, on the day of my actual Bar Mitzvah, I started putting on *tefillin* without much fanfare.

There is actually some history to the *tefillin* bag I received for my Bar Mitzvah. As mentioned, I was named for Uncle Mendel Tessler, who passed away as a young man. From the time I was a little boy, whenever I visited his family, my aunt would show me his *tefillin zekel* and say, "This will be yours. This is what you'll get for your Bar Mitzvah."

And so it was. My aunt gave me my uncle's *tefillin zekel,* which bore his and my name. I kept my *tefillin* in it from when I turned Bar Mitzvah and even took it with me to Birkenau.

Weddings were another occasion to celebrate, and I recall attending several weddings in my youth. There was one at a neighbor's house, and another that I attended with my family in the town of Moisei. That second one was also memorable because our family traveled to the town in a *fayaker,* a horse and carriage.

In those days, weddings took place at home, with the guests going out to the yard for the *chuppah.* The meal was cooked with the help of other women from the family or the neighborhood. Everyone contributed a dish or helped the family in the kitchen. Jewish musicians and a *badchan* enhanced the *simchah* with music and jokes.

Another special occasion in our home was when my mother emptied our *pushka*. We had a special Reb Meir Baal Haness *pushke* where my mother deposited some coins each week before *tzinding* the Shabbos *licht*. The Reb Meir Bal Haness *chaverim* visited periodically to pick up the money that had been collected in the *pushke*. They scheduled an appointment for their visit, and before they arrived, my mother spread a white tablecloth over the dining room table and put out cake and *eingemachts* (soft pieces of preserved summer fruits). After all, this visit was considered a very special occasion.

When the two men, friends of my father, would arrive, one would immediately take the *pushke* and begin counting out the money. Meanwhile, the second man would begin haggling with my mother. "Esther, *di hust nisht gegeiben genig gelt*," he would say. ("You did not give enough money.")

Eventually, my mother would agree to add some more money to the total to satisfy the men. They would then give her a receipt, which had a picture of Kever Rachel, as it once appeared. This piece of paper was then considered "*ah heilige zach*," a holy thing, in our home. I remember my mother admonishing us, "*Rier es nisht uhn! S'iz heilig.*" ("Don't touch it. It's holy.") After all, an illustration of a holy place in the Holy Land was not something that was looked upon lightly in a generation where visits to and pictures of Eretz Yisrael were extremely rare.

Sometimes my father was also asked to work for this *tzeddakah* fund, as well as other causes on behalf of the *kehillah*. However, my father always resisted becoming involved in *kuhlishe zachen*—things related to the *kehilla*. Whether it was the politics or commitment of time that turned him off, he always maintained that with all the travels necessary to keep finding products for his store, and the many commitments involved in raising his large family, he was not the right person to become involved.

Indeed, though he was a strict, demanding father, he was a constant, reassuring presence, always looking out for us and involved in every aspect of our lives.

Chapter Four: Gathering Storm Clouds

I was eleven or twelve years old when I first began sensing the rumblings coming from Germany. There were some radios in town, but we didn't own one. There were newspapers, too, which were delivered from Warsaw to local subscribers. Typically, these subscriptions were shared by four people, with the paper going first to the one who paid the most and then to the others. However, my father considered both radios and newspapers too modern for his strictly *chassidishe* home, and I was only vaguely aware of political developments in nearby countries. Nonetheless, by September 1940, even I knew that trouble was brewing around us.

Earlier that year, there had been rising tensions between Romania and Hungary due to a territorial dispute. Both countries gathered troops at the border, as Hungary threatened to retake large chunks of land it had lost after World War I. Eventually, Nazi Germany and Fascist Italy intervened, promising to work out an agreement, which resulted in the Second Vienna Award.

Our region was directly impacted by the Second Vienna Award, which divided Transylvania between Romania and Hungary. Hitler was looking to appease the Hungarians, and Northern Transylvania, which included all of Maramures and part of Crisana, was annexed to Hungary. Though Romania lost considerable land, they had avoided an all-out war with the Hungarians, who actually claimed the rights to an even bigger piece of land. The agreement was finalized on August 30, 1940, and over the next few weeks, Hungarian soldiers began taking over positions in our region.

I still recall the day when the Hungarian soldiers marched into Visheve. They arrived in our town on September 6, and we boys ran out of *cheder* to see what was happening. Unfortunately, their arrival did not bode well for Jewish businesses, as the soldiers closed all the stores that didn't have Hungarian licenses. Our store's license was under the name Fanny Traubkatz, my paternal grandmother's maiden name. She had opened the store decades earlier, and renewing the license now was no simple matter. The initial solution, therefore, was to continue doing business quietly. The front door to the street remained closed, but customers continued coming in through the side door. That door faced a big yard that stood between the store and our family's home. Customers rang a little bell and someone would come running from the house to serve them.

After a short while, the Hungarians also forbade Jews from attending public school and *cheder*. Instead we went to *shul*, and the *rebbes* continued teaching us there.

Around this time, we began seeing Polish Jews arriving in our town, as they tried to escape to safer regions. Visheve is only twenty-four kilometers from the Polish Galician border, so many Jews hid in our town for a couple of days before continuing to Budapest with false documents. Any Romanian harboring refugees with these documents was accused of spying and immediately shot dead, so it was quite dangerous to help these escapees. Nonetheless, a number of Jews, including the Bobover and Belzer Rebbes, survived by escaping through this route, going from Poland to Slovakia and then on to Budapest.

Though no Germans were stationed in Visheve, groups of German soldiers sometimes passed our town. Whenever they did, they would walk into our store, as well as other stores, and demand items from the shelves. Afterwards, they would leave without paying a cent, and there was nothing we could do about it. This also occurred in Uncle Baruch's store in the main Jewish area. Rivka Fireworker, a sister of Baruch's wife Ekka, was in her early twenties at the time and working in the store. There, too, the soldiers demanded a number of items and walked out.

By the middle of 1943, our situation had drastically worsened. We could no longer walk outside without a yellow star. *Shechitah* was soon also prohibited, and the Hungarian aggressors closed down the Jewish slaughterhouse.

After the law prohibiting *shechitah* was passed, Jews were able to get away with killing fowl at night, because the authorities could not control what was happening in people's yards. However, it was much harder to *shecht* heifers, cows, or goats in secret, so it was difficult for us to obtain meat.

Luckily, our cousin Meir was a butcher in the next town of Ruscova (or Riskeve in Yiddish), about fourteen kilometers, or nine miles, north of Visheve. Meir was a cousin by marriage, as he had married Tilla, the daughter of my father's sister Faiga. Though Meir's butcher shop was no longer open, he was still able to procure meat and arranged with my father to send some.

My parents were afraid to send my older brothers to pick up the meat, since young men were regularly taken off the streets and drafted for forced labor. Thus, it fell to me, the oldest of the younger children, to pick up the meat from Meir.

I was a young boy then, around thirteen years old, and I nervously caught the afternoon train to Ruscova. At around two or three o'clock in the morning, I went with Meir and the town's *shochet* to a barn in his yard. Meir closed the door tightly, and working by the light of a kerosene lamp, the *shochet* proceeded to slaughter a cow right in front of us. Afterwards, Meir worked quickly to remove the skin and the *shochet* was *bodek* the lungs. The whole process took no more than

fifteen minutes. Meir then began cutting the meat into smaller pieces and wrapped a piece of meat for my family. He helped me hide it
against my chest, and I remember being surprised by how warm the
meat felt. Since it was in the middle of the winter, we hoped my jacket
would hide the meat well until I arrived home the next morning.

Several hours later, I went to catch the early morning train back
to Visheve. However, a sharp-eyed gendarme, as we called the local
policemen, noticed my rather clumsy gait. "What have you got there?"
he called. I was too afraid to lie, and naively admitted the truth.

In our town, there were two train stations: the *kleine shtantzion*
(small station) at the beginning of town, near where we lived, and the
groise shtantzion (large station), which was a kilometer or two away,
in the center of town, and connected to several other lines. My father
was waiting for me at the first station, but the policeman took me to
the center of town. When my father saw that I wasn't at the station, he
realized right away that I was in trouble. He hurried into town, and
before long, he found me. In typical Romanian fashion, he was able
to pay a bribe and take me home, though I think the meat stayed with
the police.

With time, it became more and more dangerous for young men
to walk the streets. Besides for official labor groups that were formed,
soldiers sometimes snatched people at random to complete some
work. For example, when there was a fire up in the mountains once,
Hungarian soldiers grabbed Jewish men off the street to go fight the
fire. Another time—I think this was during the winter of 1943—there
was a rumor in town that the soldiers were preparing to snatch people
for another work assignment. This was during the *matzah* baking season, when men were working in the bakery around the clock. Since
people were afraid to leave their homes, the bakery manager recruited
young boys like me and my brothers to help out all night at the *matzah*
bakery.

As the Hungarians became more organized, the drafting of men became more systematic. Since they didn't want Jewish men serving in the army, they drafted them instead for slave labor groups, known as *munkataber*. The Jewish units were stationed all over Hungary, as well as in the Eastern Front in Ukraine, and were treated with extreme cruelty. They were badly fed and poorly clothed, and many were killed without provocation. Some entire units were wiped out, and those who survived often returned crippled and broken.

My father's youngest brother, Uncle Baruch, was one of the men taken to *munkataber*. The Hungarians had ordered all able-bodied men under the age of thirty-five or forty, who had fewer than five children, to report for slave labor. Since my father had nine children, he was exempt, but Baruch, who had only four, was taken to *munkataber*. Tragically, he never met a fifth child, a baby boy who was born after he had been drafted.

My uncle's battalion, number 108/4, was stationed in Tisa-Ojleg in Hungary. They were then taken to Ukraine, behind German lines, and ordered to dig trenches and do other difficult, manual labor.

In Ukraine, the battalion was stationed in a town called Doroshitza. There was a field hospital that had been organized in a large stable, and all who were weak or sick were able to go to the hospital to rest up. In April of 1943, Erev Shabbos HaGadol, my uncle felt terribly weak and wanted to go to the hospital. Some men tried to dissuade him, telling him that there were rumors that the soldiers were going to liquidate the hospital. In his weakened state, Baruch felt that he had no choice. Sensing that he would not survive, he gave away whatever food he had left to his friends and stumbled towards the stable.

Sure enough, a group of Hungarian soldiers soon surrounded the hospital and sealed all the exits with boards and nails. Then, on Friday night, Shabbos HaGadol, they spread gasoline around the stable and torched it. Whoever tried to break through the windows or jump out was assaulted with a barrage of machine gun fire.

Tragically, there were about 800 young men, most of them in their twenties or thirties from in and around the Visheves, who were burned alive on that day. I have not seen this story recorded anywhere and want this terrible event to be remembered for history.[4]

When news of our uncle's tragic death reached the Visheves, my father initially tried to protect Baruch's wife Ekka, who was his niece as well as his sister-in-law, and did not immediately tell her what happened. She was trying to manage the household on her own and care for her five children: a daughter Malka, two sons, Chaim and Shlomo Ber, another child whose name I do not remember, and a newborn baby. Fortunately, her sister Rivka was there, helping her manage the store and care for her family. My father was also involved, having arranged for a *rebbe* to learn with Chaim and Shlomo Ber and ultimately helping them say Kaddish for their father.

Some months after our uncle's death, my family suffered another loss. One day, Baruch and I were taking care of *Der Zeide* in his room. We were feeding him *koilish* in *kava*, or *challah* softened in coffee. I held the plate as Baruch slowly fed our grandfather. Suddenly, my grandfather made an unusual, throaty sound and then passed away right in front of our eyes. The room had a large window that faced the store. We knocked urgently to alert our father. He came running quickly, but it was already over. My grandfather was eighty-eight when he was *niftar* on 7 Shvat, 1943.

It is interesting to note that when anyone passed away in the Visheves, one or two spoonfuls of earth from Eretz Yisrael were buried with the *niftar*. If the person had been a rich man, a pillow of this earth was formed underneath his head. This was considered a *segulah* for making the journey to Eretz Yisrael easier during *techias hameisim*.

---

4   Some years ago, I met a Yid who was visiting the United States from Eretz Yisrael and had come to a *shul* in my neighborhood. He recounted that his wife's grandfather lived in the Bronx and had also been in *munkataber*, in another platoon in this region. That Bronx man had also been inside the stable when it was set on fire, and he managed to jump out of a window together with some others. Though most of them were hit by machine gun fire, he was one of the few who managed to escape unharmed. He said that for seven or eight days afterwards, the smell of burning flesh hung in the air.

After *Der Zeide's* passing, things kept growing progressively worse in Visheve. By early spring of 1944, the situation was quite serious. We spent the last few weeks together as a family in our own home in Nissan of 5704. Pesach fell early in April that year and ended on the fifteenth. Shortly afterwards, during the last week of April, we suddenly received orders to take our belongings and move uptown, to the *Yiddishe Gas*, the main Jewish street in Oyber-Visheve.

I was fourteen and a half years old at the time. My youngest brother, Moishy, was almost four and had received his first haircut less than a year earlier. Our beautiful family was never to be the same again.

We called the Hungarian gendarmes "feathers" because they had chicken feathers in their helmets. The day that we were to leave our homes, we suddenly spotted them coming up our street. "The feathers are here! The feathers are coming!" we cried.

The gendarmes went from house to house and soon arrived at our home too. "You have an hour to pack up. You're going to the ghetto," they announced.

My father got a horse and wagon and began loading up some of our belongings, as we children stood outside and watched. Suddenly, we saw our German neighbor Raiza appear in the yard.

Raiza lived about five houses down with her husband and family and regularly shopped at our store. Typically, my father would record amounts owed in a book, and customers would settle their accounts every few weeks. Whenever one book was filled, my father would begin recording charges and payments in a new one. Raiza was one of those customers who still owed money from the "old book," yet my father continued serving her.

Now, as my parents were anxiously packing up, Raiza went into our house and began taking things out. "What are you doing?" my mother cried. "These are our things! You are stealing!"

"No," she replied defiantly. "You are not coming back here anymore. You don't need these things. If someone else is going to have them, it may as well be me!"

We looked on in shock but could do nothing. Soon after, as we climbed into the wagon, the policemen went to seal our house. "It's for your protection," they said. "So that nothing will be touched while you're in the ghetto."

We were fortunate that Uncle Baruch's home was located within the ghetto, so at least we had a place to go. We were very close with Aunt Ekka and her family, so the house was familiar to us, making the transition a little easier. However, we were far from comfortable, as families from many surrounding towns were brought to the new ghetto and we shared the house with the families of my father's sisters, Faiga from Moisei and Yenta from Borsa. The house was terribly over-crowded, with uncles, aunts, and cousins, and we children slept across the floors of the house and in the attic.

As hard as it was, we knew that we had it easier than many others. After all, thousands of Jews (more than 15,000, I believe) had been forced into the Vişeu de Sus Ghetto, which took up only a fraction of the original Jewish neighborhood. Many remained homeless and had no place to go.

The ghetto was enclosed with barbed wire and was guarded by the Hungarian police. Though there were bread rations, food was not dis-tributed regularly. Our supplies were soon almost completely depleted, though we were fortunate to have a well in the yard. A committee was formed to find some solutions, but I was too young to follow all the de-velopments. I know some people managed to obtain passes to leave the ghetto for short periods. Additionally, the local hospital had its back entrance inside the ghetto and its front entrance outside. There was some kind of system with people occasionally sneaking out from there.

Unlike Polish ghettoes, no Jews were murdered in ours. Quite sim-ply, our ghetto existed for so few weeks that there wasn't much time for anything to happen. Almost immediately, the first transport went off with about 4,000 people.

Families taken on the first transport were those who had nowhere to sleep and had been out on the streets. The second transport, which followed soon after, also contained mostly out-of-towners. The third transport, which was the one my family went on, was filled with local townspeople. A fourth one followed soon after, taking the rest of the residents, including all the prominent people who had managed to postpone leaving until then. After this final transport, there were no Jews left in the Visheves.

My parents had some prior warning before our departure and were able to prepare provisions for our family. My mother and aunt prepared a high-calorie food, called *shtolwerk* in Hungarian, which they had also sent to Uncle Baruch for nourishment after he was taken to *munkataber*. *Shtolwerk* was cubes of hardened caramel that were formed after cooking a mixture of milk and sugar overnight, for ten or twelve hours. They also made fresh noodles, in which they put in extra eggs for additional nourishment. Afterwards, they prepared for every child a rucksack with a change of clothes and the caramel cubes and noodles. They told us that we would be able to put these cubes in some milk or eat them as is and that they would provide nourishment equal to a day's worth of food.

Before our departure, each child put on two pairs of underwear and clothing so that we would have enough clothes to wear. Then, we received our rucksack, containing precious provisions for survival.

We were taken to the trains on Sunday, May 21, 1944, a little more than three weeks after arriving at the ghetto. As we left the house, I remember my father holding two books under his arms, the *alte bich* and the *neieh bich*. These books, which were the last two books of his customers' outstanding accounts, essentially held the records of his entire fortune.

We were marched toward the train station and forced to board the train, about seventy or eighty people per wagon. The doors were sealed shut, and then at nightfall, the trains started moving out.

The Hungarian soldiers told us that we were being taken to a farm community in Hungary, where able-bodied men would work while the women and children cooked and took care of the household. They explained that we were being evacuated because the Russian front was approaching, so it was necessary to move us deeper into Hungary.

By then, the adults knew that there were German camps for Jews in Poland. I overheard them saying that the train would first have to go to Košice (or Kasho in Yiddish, which was then part of Hungary), where there was a central train station. If the train then turned left, they said, it would be going into Hungary, as the soldiers claimed. However, if it turned right from Košice, then we were heading towards Slovakia and Poland, towards the German camps.

When the train pulled into the central station at Košice, we all waited with bated breath, anxious to see what would happen. While we were there, the Hungarian soldiers suddenly left and SS soldiers took control of the train. When it began moving again, it turned right as it departed the station. The adults became very tense, realizing that we were indeed heading towards the German camps, and not towards a safe haven in Hungary.

Some people wonder why we didn't act, why we didn't try to tear the barbed wires from the windows, jump out, and run away. What they don't realize is that we were *trapped,* whether inside or outside the train. Where could we possibly have escaped to? Where could we find shelter and safety? The entire region was controlled by madmen. There was nowhere and no one to run to.

Thus, for three days we rode on that train, heading towards the worst hell created by humans on earth. All we could do was *daven* to Hashem and hope that He would protect us.

CHAPTER FIVE:
FACES IN THE FLAMES

O ur transport from the ghetto in Vişeu de Sus pulled into the Auschwitz-Birkenau station at around noon. I believe the date was Wednesday, May 24, 1944. There were many trains already in the station, and the doors on ours remained locked while the Nazis dealt with transports that had arrived before ours.

Before we got off the train, a remarkable incident occurred. There was another train waiting on the line parallel to ours, and people called out to each other to see where that train was from and who was on it. Incredibly, my parents discovered that our grandfather from Vilchovitz, whom we saw very infrequently, was on the wagon directly opposite ours!

The wagons had four windows, high up on the wall at each corner, covered with barbed wire. If we climbed onto each other, we were able to peek out of the train. As soon as my mother realized that her father was on the next train, she turned over a big pot and climbed onto it. Thanks to this incredible turn of events, my mother was able to have a conversation for several minutes with her father, Shmiel Chaim Rosenfeld, who was eighty-six years old at the time and had come from the ghetto in Munkatch. Through incredible *hashgachah pratis*, the two had a final conversation before they were sent to the gas chambers.

Eventually, the other train was moved away and ours remained alone on the tracks. Finally, just as the sky was turning dark, the doors opened up. There was a lot of noise and much commotion. All the train doors had been opened at once, and people everywhere were streaming out of the wagons as commands were barked at us. "Out! Out! Out! Quickly! Everyone out! Drop your things! Leave everything behind!"

The scene was one of terror and confusion, as we were chased out by Jews from the *Kanada-kommando*. They had arrived in Birkenau a year or two earlier and were now hardened to the daily scenes at the station. They were focused on their job: getting everyone off the trains, having all packages and valises left in piles at the station, and then sorting them all in the *Kanada* warehouse.[5]

As I stepped off—or rather was pushed off—the trains, one of the *Kanada* men looked at me and asked, "How old are you?"

"Fourteen," I replied.

"No, you're sixteen!" he said.

I had no time to dwell on our exchange as I was pushed forward by the crowd. I followed orders and dropped my sack on the growing pile of bags and suitcases. Inside that sack were my most precious possessions: my *tefillin* and the *tefillin zekel* that had belonged to Uncle Mendel. I would never see them again.

In all the tumult, I suddenly lost sight of my parents and siblings and found myself only with my older brother Baruch. We were holding hands so as not to lose each other and together we followed commands to go forward. Suddenly, we found ourselves in front of two or three German officers. One of them stood with his fingers stuck between the

---

5   The Kanada-kommando was a work unit responsible for collecting the possessions left by the Jews at the station of Auschwitz-Birkenau and taking them back to the Kanada warehouse. There, everything was sorted and prepared for transport to Germany.

To the inmates, Canada was a country that symbolized wealth, and the name seemed to fit the facility, which was filled with clothing, jewelry, and other valuables left by Jews. The name stuck, and not only was it used to refer to the warehouse, but by extension, to that section of the camp and to the group of people who worked there.

buttons of his jacket, only his thumb exposed at his chest. I would later learn that he was the notorious doctor of Auschwitz-Birkenau, Josef Mengele, the Angel of Death.

"*Buba* (boy), how old are you?" he asked me.

The words of that *Kanada* worker suddenly echoed in my mind. "Sixteen!" I said. I was tall for my age and hoped that my lie was believable.

He moved his thumb a centimeter or two, pointing me to the right. Before I could move, he turned to Baruch and said, "*Buba,* how old are you?"

"Eighteen!" he replied. (He had actually turned 16 only two months earlier.)

He motioned again to the right, and before we could follow his instructions, we were shoved in that direction. We continued following the others in the semi-darkness, when we suddenly spotted our father and oldest brother Tuli.

"Why aren't you going over there?" my father asked me, pointing to where the women with young children stood on the other side. "You should go with your mother! Someone will have to help her with the children."

At the time, my father still believed that the women would be cooking and caring for the children. He was concerned that my mother would have a difficult time with all the little ones and wanted me to help her.

"I don't want to go," I said.

"So Baruch, you go!" my father said, turning to my brother.

Seeing how adamant my father was, the two of us moved back a bit, but we remained with our group. I cannot explain why we didn't listen to our father. We were very obedient children who usually followed our father's every command without thinking. Somehow, though, our instincts told us to remain where we were and that's what we did. In fact, this wouldn't be the last time that our instincts would tell us to behave in ways we could not explain, ultimately saving our lives.

Throughout this time, there was much chaos and screaming around us. At one point, there seemed to be quite a commotion in one particular area, but with all the yelling, we couldn't see what had happened. After the war, I learned the story behind all that noise.

I had a cousin who was about twenty years old at the time. She was the daughter of Yenta from Borsa, and her name was Malka Mendelovitch. Yenta had no children for twelve years, until she finally gave birth to Malka, and then to a son, Shmiel Yida.

During the commotion, Malka started running away and was shot by SS officers. She wasn't immediately killed, but was writhing on the ground in pain, screaming "Kill me! Kill me!" The Nazis gathered all the women around her and warned them that anyone else who tried to escape would be shot like her. After finishing the speech, the Nazis shot at her again. She was the first person to die from our transport. (None of my family members ever found Shmiel Yida after the war, so we assume that, tragically, both Yenta's children perished during the Holocaust.)

While all this was happening, our group starting marching away from the trains. Suddenly, a number of floodlights went on, and the area was lit up like in the middle of the day.

We didn't know it at the time, but we were being marched toward Camp G in Birkenau. Birkenau, which the Germans sometimes called Auschwitz Tzvei (Two), consisted of camps A through G. The showers were located in Camp G, and beyond them, the crematoriums.

We arrived at Camp G shortly before midnight. It was quite cool outside, but we were told to undress completely and only take our shoes and belts with us. Everything else had to be left behind.

We were taken to a big room and told that our hair would be cut and we would then be showered and dressed. We lined up as ordered, and Jewish inmates began cutting our hair with old-fashioned, non-electric cutters. More often than not, as they sheared off beards and hair, the barbers took off skin from the face and scalp too. Perhaps the blades were too dull, or they were being ordered to work too quickly, but regardless of the reason, screams soon filled the room as the new arrivals endured painful haircuts.

As we stood in line, we were treated to snide remarks from some of the Jewish barbers. "You've had it good for a long time, eh?" some of them asked. "It's time for you to start suffering too," others said. "We've been here two years already!" It was quite clear that these tormented, bitter Jews were not particularly sympathetic to us, "lucky" people who had only just arrived.

After our haircuts, we were taken to the showers. Large groups of people were shoved into the rooms, until they were completely full. The water felt oily, and we came out with some unusual odor cling-ing to our skin, probably from some disinfectant that was put into the water.

By now, Baruch and I were once again reunited with our father and Tuli, and the four of us stuck together as we were led to another room. It was brutally cold, since it was in the middle of the night and we were standing naked outside, wet from the showers.

Finally, each of us received a pair of pants and a shirt. We were told to stay in the area and remained there until daybreak. We were guarded by *häftlinge*, fellow inmates, while the SS stood off to the side.

It took a while for the entire transport to be processed, for ev-eryone to be shorn, showered, and dressed. We waited there for a few hours until everyone was ready. Finally, our entire group was marched out of G Lager.

It is difficult to envision the size of the camp. Birkenau, which was built as an extension to Auschwitz, held tens of thousands of people. As we marched down a main road, away from the crematoriums, we passed gates leading into the other *lagers*. Each *lager* had a long road running through it, with barracks lined up on either side. The road was set up like a regular neighborhood block, with even-numbered barracks on one side and odd-numbered barracks on the other. There were about thirty *blocks*, or barracks, in each *lager*, and each *block* housed close to 1,000 people, and sometimes even more.

When we reached C Lager, the gate was opened and we turned into the C road. It was quite overwhelming marching down that long road with barracks on either side. C Lager was mixed at the time, and we saw some *blocks* containing men and others women. C Lager would only be a temporary home for us, and we stayed there no more than two or three days.

When we were finally brought inside one of the barracks, we found bunk beds three or four levels high. Ten or twelve people were expected to share each bunk, and some slept on the floor for lack of space.

At the far end of the barracks, on a small platform beyond a couple of steps, stood two large barrels, which inmates used to relieve themselves. This area was open, allowing for no privacy at all. The Nazis used every opportunity to degrade us and remove any shred of human dignity. With typical efficiency, they put a *kommando* in charge of these barrels, the *Sheiss-kommando*. Members of this *kommando* were assigned the unpleasant task of going around the camp each day with wheelbarrows to empty the barrels.

As I looked around the barracks, tears kept falling from my eyes. Though I was with my father and two brothers, I could not stop crying.

"Why are you crying?" my father asked.

"I'm hungry," I told him.

My father went out, hoping to organize[6] something for me. He fi-

---

6   In the camps, "organize" was a euphemism for steal or trade. One couldn't survive without "organizing" some extra food or finding a way to procure extra clothes in exchange for cigarettes or other valued items. Of course, if anyone was caught, the offender would be

nally returned with a small piece of bread. However, it was so hard that I couldn't eat it and gave it back to him. At last, we received bowls and were served a thick black coffee. Only about half a cup was splashed into each person's bowl, and it tasted more like mud than coffee. Nonetheless, with nothing else to quiet our hunger, the inmates lined up for the coffee.

When my father handed me a bowl with coffee, I burst into tears again. "Why are you crying now?" he asked.

"I want *Di Mamme* to give me the food," I said.

I carried on like that by each feeding, not quite ready to be the brave young boy I'd need to be to survive in that nightmarish place.

It didn't take long for us to learn what had happened to my dear mother and younger siblings. As we settled in and spoke with other inmates, we learned that the fires we had seen, some two or three feet tall, were coming from the crematoriums, where most of our transport had been taken. My poor mother was only thirty-nine years old when she was murdered together with six of her children on 3 Sivan, 1944.

The inmates depended on dark humor to survive in the camp. It was the only way to remain sane in our mad world. Thus, they dubbed the crematorium "*di pipkele fabric*," or the pipe factory. "By tomorrow we'll surely be going to the *pipkele fabric*," they'd tell each other.

They also amused themselves by finding faces in the flames. Sometimes they imagined they saw an image of a face with a long beard and declared that a *chashuve rebbe* had just passed through the chimney. Other times they'd make out the silhouette of a woman holding a child.

Survival in the camp depended not only on learning how to joke about death but also learning the camp's operating systems. We soon learned that Birkenau had three primary purposes. It was a ***concentrazia lager***, a ***handles lager***, and a ***toitens lager***. *Concentrazia lager*, or

---

beaten or killed.

arbeits lager, means that it was a place where some inmates were kept alive to work. *Handels lager* means that it was a place where prisoners were *handeled*, or traded, for a certain price. German-owned companies in the surrounding areas were able to take new arrivals as slave laborers. The owners or managers would come to the camp and request 1,000 workers, 5,000 workers, or as many as they needed. Prisoners thus kept leaving the camp on *kommandos*, labor units that were sent to satellite camps nearby or to factories and other work sites in the surrounding areas. Since prisoners were then cared for and fed by their new guardians, conditions weren't the same everywhere, and some inmates fared better and some worse. Finally, Birkenau's main purpose was to serve as a *toitens lager*, a death camp, or *farnichtungs* (liquidation) camp, where Zyklon B gas was used to murder large groups of people at a time in four massive gas chambers.[7]

We also quickly became familiar with the many terms that were used to refer to those with authority in the camp. In each *lager*, there was a *blockalteste*, a person in charge of the entire *block*; a *shtube-dinst*, the assistant, who was responsible for the cleanliness and order of the barrack; and a *schreiber*, the secretary who kept a record of how many inmates were in the barrack.

In Birkenau, there were many lengthy *appels*,[8] sometimes several times each day. In addition to the regular *appel* before the distribution of food, there were also repeat *selektzias*. Each time, inmates who had become weak or ill were separated and sent to the gas chambers.

Several days after our arrival, I think this was the second day of Shavuous or the day after Shavuous, everyone under sixteen was ordered to step out of the *block*. Supposedly, we would be assigned to easier work than the adults.

---

7 According to Yad Vashem estimates, more than 1,200,000 people were gassed in Auschwitz-Birkenau. This figure includes about 1,100,000 Jews, 70,000 Poles, 25,000 Sinti and Roma Gypsies, and some 15,000 prisoners of war from the USSR and other countries.

8 *Appels* were daily roll calls. Officially, they were intended to count the inmates, but they were also used to weaken and humiliate them.

I didn't want to go and very few other children went. When the *blockalteste* saw that no one was going, he had the *schreiber* draw up a list of all the children. The list had a total of one hundred and one names, including mine.

When the names were announced, all the children had to line up in the yard. We stepped into formation and were ordered to begin marching out together. As we marched away from the *block*, I left behind my father and brothers, who had provided a measure of comfort and security until then. I would no longer see any of them until after the war.

Within a few days, my father and brothers were taken to serve in a *kommando* that was assigned to work in Warsaw and eventually to clean up the Warsaw Ghetto, a grisly task which brought them face to face with piles of skeletons that had been left in streets and bunkers. This was after the Warsaw Ghetto Uprising, and the Germans specifically chose Hungarian Jews for the unit because they didn't know the region or language and would not be able to escape. It was a large *kommando* of several thousand Hungarian Jews, including the holy Klausenberger Rebbe, Rabbi Yekusiel Yehudah Halberstam, *zt"l*, who inspired inmates with his strong faith. After the war, he would immigrate to New York and later to Israel, where he established the Sanz-Klausenburg *chassidus* in Netanya. There, he also famously built the non-profit Laniado Hospital, fulfilling a vow he had made after being grazed by a bullet during the death march.

One might assume that after our separation I thought of my father and brothers constantly. That was not the case. When you are stuck in a place like Birkenau, you begin to think only of yourself. You don't think of your family or of anything happening around you. Instead, you live minute by minute: *In this particular instant, will I get my breath? Will I survive today? Tonight, will the lice eat me up? Will I get clubbed to death?* At night, you worry what will happen in the morning, and in the morning, you worry what will happen at night: *Will I get my food? Will I starve? Will Mengele take me out?*

True, I had been crying constantly beforehand, but after our separation, I had to look out for myself and did not think of my father and brothers at all. Instead, I became consumed with the particulars of survival.

After I was marched off together with the other children, our group was initially taken to join other children in A Lager. We were now 900 young boys in all, and after a day or two, we were all transferred to D Lager. We were divided into two groups of 450, each group assigned to a different *block* in D Lager. We were told that we would soon be taken to Germany to be trained as brick layer foremen.

D Lager was the *arbeits-lager* of Birkenau. Everyone in D Lager was part of a *kommando* that worked inside the camp. *Blocks* 11 and 13, and perhaps also 9, housed the men of the infamous *Sonderkommando*. They had the horrific job of collecting the corpses of the people who had been gassed, extracting gold teeth, removing valuables, and then taking them to the crematoriums to be burned.

At first glance, members of the *Sonderkommando* fared better than anyone else in the camp. They received better food and had easy access to other supplies. Nonetheless, no one wished to work in this unit. Besides for the horror of dealing with the corpses, and sometimes coming across bodies of loved ones, being assigned to the *Sonderkommando* was actually a death sentence. Every three months or so, the entire *kommando*, with few exceptions, was thrown into the gas chambers, burned and replaced by a new group of people. In fact, the first task of each new *kommando* was to deal with the bodies of the previous one. These men had seen too much and the Nazis did not want them to be left alive to share the horrors that they'd witnessed.[9]

The food in D Camp was better than in other parts of the camp. As

---

9   Knowing that certain death awaited them, a group of men from the *Sonderkommando*,
     including Jewish inmates and Russian prisoners of war, staged a revolt several months
     later, in October of 1944. They managed to kill three SS officers and wound several others.
     Though some inmates escaped, eventually all were found and killed. Nonetheless, the revolt
     was not a complete failure. During the operation, the inmates had destroyed the Birkenau
     crematoriums, which were never used again.

in other *lagers,* we received coffee in the morning and bread at night. However, here we were also treated to a sweet paste resembling farina once or twice a week. Sometimes we also got our hands on a piece of chocolate or soap. The better food was either meant to make us strong for our upcoming work or was simply the reality of living in D Lager.

The men from D Lager took pity on us children and tried to smuggle food and other goods to us. Though we weren't allowed to leave our *block,* we sometimes sneaked into other *blocks* and found extra food. Sometimes the men gave us their shoes to polish and left packages of food inside for us to find. Those who worked in the *Kanadakommando* would bring food and other things they found while sorting through clothing, eyeglasses, shoes, and other items.

Several days after arriving in the camp, I asked one of the old timers, "*Vi azoi geit men arois fin danen?*" ("How does one get out of here?")

The man pointed his finger towards the billowing crematorium chimney. "*Fin du geit men arois durechen koimen,*" he answered. ("From here you leave through the chimney.")

His ominous words would haunt me for the rest of my stay in that camp. I was determined to prove him wrong and walk out of Birkenau on my own two feet.

After four weeks, there was an outbreak of typhus in the neighboring *block* and we were moved back to A Lager. While we waited for the other children to recover, there was a typhus outbreak by us too. We were quarantined by Dr. Mengele, who came every day to examine us and monitor the situation

Whenever Mengele came in to inspect us, he would say, "*Vus machen meine yugent?*" ("How are my youngsters doing?")

We were his special project, future slaves who could work for many years as bricklayers of the Thousand-Year Reich. Incredibly, while he could speak so affectionately to us, we were still mere cogs in the machine of the Third Reich. We received very little food in A Camp and many of us became very thin. Each time he came, Mengele would motion for anyone who looked too gaunt or weak to step aside. With cold-blooded efficiency, he would regularly select five or ten children, who would immediately be marched off to the crematoriums.

The typhus outbreaks prompted a change of plans, and the Nazis abandoned the plan to take us to Germany. The future of our shrinking group of young boys seemed uncertain, but I refused to accept that my only route of escape was through the chimney. I was determined as ever to keep my wits about me and survive another day.

Chapter Six: Summer in Hell

S ummer came to Birkenau, just as it did to the rest of the world. Though we welcomed the sun's bright, warm rays, they seemed misplaced in our dark, cold world. There could be no sense of optimism or renewal here. Quite the opposite; I was often only thirty meters from the crematoriums and kept an anxious eye on the flames, which seemed to be leaping towards the sky with ever greater frequency. Time and again, entire *blocks* of people disappeared right in front of our eyes.

There were several thousand Russian soldiers, prisoners of war, who lived with us in A Lager. While we were in the higher number *blocks*, in the twenties, they were in the lower barracks, but still in the same camp. One night, towards the end of July, the soldiers were lined up at night. We heard them marching and singing for some time. Then, in the middle of the night, we suddenly heard a number of trucks coming into A Lager. The singing stopped, and after a while, the trucks left and everything was quiet again.

A short time later, there were big flames going up from the crematorium. The fire continued burning for hours, and word in the camp was that all those Russian soldiers had been taken to the crematoriums.

Soon afterwards, we witnessed the disappearance of another large group of inmates. At the time, there were Czechoslovakian families who were living together in B Lager. We often watched from afar as family members conversed and little children played on bikes. Then, one evening in the middle of August, we had a *blocksperre,* a lockdown. No one was permitted to leave the barracks.

As we sat inside our *block,* we suddenly heard a lot of noise coming from the Czech *lager.* We moved towards the back of the barracks, to the large door behind the barrels that inmates used to relieve themselves. That door had some cracks in it, and though we couldn't see much, it was clear that there was something happening in B Lager. Later, we saw large flames coming from the distance, and it was clear that the crematoriums were working full force.

In the morning, when we went outside, we found B Lager completely deserted. We saw wheelchairs, bicycles, and other abandoned items, but the people were all gone.

After the Czech families were taken away, B Lager became a women's camp. We called out sometimes to the girls in the neighboring *lager,* looking for family members and friends. One day, I found my cousins Ratzi and Esther Tessler, the children of my Uncle Mendel, for whom I had been named.[10]

At some point during the summer, we were told that we would be moved to the *Tziganer Lager,* which had housed the Roma (Gypsies) and was actually the F Lager, close to the crematoriums. Though their camp had been recently liquidated and no Gypsies were there anymore, we continued calling it the *Tziganer Lager.*

Before our move, Mengele examined everyone and then spoke quietly to the *blockalteste.* We received our bread early that day, and after we ate, the *blockalteste* ordered us to line up.

We stood there for a long time, waiting to be transferred. We became very nervous because we were afraid that we would actually be

---

10   Fortunately, both survived the war and later immigrated to New York. Ratzi married Mendel Potasnik and Esther married Shimon Kopolowitz. Two other sisters, Sura and Montzy (her real name was Malka) both died after the liberation. Montzy perished in Bergen-Belsen after eating poisoned bread that killed thousands of survivors in the days after they were freed. Sura passed away in Sweden in a resort area, where she had traveled with her two surviving sisters, after the Swedes allowed some survivors to enter to recuperate there after the war.

taken to the crematoriums. We started saying goodbye to each other and preparing for the worst.

Finally, we were counted and led out of the camp. When we approached the F Lager, Mengele stood by the gate and gave us a speech, telling us about the importance of hygiene and that anyone who could not stay clean would be taken out.

F Camp had become the new center for Jewish arrivals and was terribly overcrowded, with as many as one thousand or twelve hundred people in each *block*. We were split into groups of one hundred and taken into different barracks to squeeze into whatever tiny space was left. After this move, our group of boys was no longer kept separated and we were mixed together with the general male population.

Because of the congestion in the barracks, going to sleep required a coordinated effort, which was executed under the watchful eye of the *blockalteste*. Everyone on the bunk had to sit down together, each person between the legs of the one behind him. It was impossible to turn over in middle of the night, and if anyone had to get up, he could not return to his place until the next morning. With time, as men were picked out to be sent to the crematoriums or to join a *kommando*, the congestion was eased a bit, but we still had to wake up our neighbor if we wanted to turn over at night.

In August, the death machines at Birkenau worked almost nonstop. Many Hungarian transports kept arriving at the camp, as well as the last residents of the liquidated Łódź Ghetto. Tragically, most of the new arrivals were gassed immediately. On August 28, Chaim Mordechai Rumkowski arrived. He was the powerful and arrogant leader of the *Judenrat* in the Łódź Ghetto. A ruthless tyrant who had been appointed by the Nazis, Rumkowski was despised by the Jews in the ghetto, who mockingly called him "King Chaim." In fact, his name appeared on special currency that was printed and used in the ghetto. Word in the camp was that he had been driven from the train to the *Kanada* complex in a Red Cross station wagon. According to some accounts, he was beaten to death by members of the *Sonderkommando*, while others say he was thrown alive into the fires of the crematorium.

As transport after transport brought starving people with their final possessions, the camp suddenly had an influx of clothing, personal items, and even sewing machines, adding to the German's ever-growing stockpiles. Each day, large numbers of the people who had been kept alive were taken away to different satellite camps and work sites. Word in Birkenau was that most *kommandos* were taken to coal mines in the area, where most didn't survive more than three or four months due to the grueling work and harsh working conditions.

Since leaving on *kommandos* appeared to be an almost certain death sentence, I was relieved that I was able to remain in the camp. Of course, there was constant danger there too. Many succumbed to illness or hunger, but I hoped that I would somehow survive. My biggest fears were getting picked out during a *selektzia* or inadvertently angering one of the Nazis and being severely punished. Somehow, as hard as we tried to stay out of trouble, each day posed new challenges.

In each *lager*, the administrative quarters, including the kitchen and office, were in *Block 1*. My friends and I were in the higher number *blocks*, in the twenties. Each day, some of us were sent to the kitchen to pick up three or four heavy thirty-gallon drums that were filled with food for our *block*. The drums had two handles, like upside down U's, and two long poles were put through them. Each drum was carried by four people, two in the front and two in the back, each of them holding one end of a pole. Those who carried the drums were able to lick them out on the return trip, and these few extra spoonfuls of food were often a matter of survival. For this reason, many were eager to take the job of carrying the drums.

One day, I was selected with three others to pick up the food. We were all quite short, and my friends and I had trouble lifting the tall, heavy drum off the ground. As we started walking, the bottom of the drum struck a stone and a quart or two of soup spilled out.

As we adjusted the drum and were about to continue walking, an SS officer yelled out, "Halt!"

Drawing his gun, he asked sharply, "Do you know what you did? You dumped food on the floor!"

The four of us played dumb, pretending not to have noticed the spilled soup. The Nazi ordered us to put down the drum and go back into the kitchen. There was a large vat of water inside that was used to wash potatoes. He told us to bend over the tub, and each of us received ten blows. Next, he picked us up by our feet and dumped us into the water headfirst. We barely had a chance to take a breath before we realized what was happening. For a moment, I thought I would drown. We were still receiving blows and it was difficult to figure out where the top of the water was. Fortunately, we made it out, bloody and sputtering, as we tried to catch our breath.

We ran back outside, and as we reached for the drum again, the Nazi yelled, "Hold it up high!" We strained to pick it up high enough, and fortunately, this time we were able to walk away from *Block 1* without incident. Later, we found out that all our troubles were for naught. The soup was so thin that day that there was nothing to scrape out from the bottom of the drum.

Another time, I was overtaken by terrible stomach spasms as I carried food back to our *block*. I don't know if they were caused by hunger or by the strain of lifting the heavy drum. All I know is that I collapsed to the ground and curled up in a ball, overtaken by terrible pain.

There was a shallow ditch that ran alongside the road that we walked on. The electric wire that encircled our camp was built in the center of this narrow ditch. As soon as anyone touched the wire, there would be a sudden spark and the person became immediately charred. In fact, I had witnessed such terrible deaths on several occasions. Once, a boy's sister threw a piece of bread over the wires. He ran to the ditch to pick it up, but in his eagerness to grab the food, he became entangled in the wires. In a moment, he was torched and became completely black. Whenever the wire was touched, an alarm would sound, and the Nazis would come see what happened and order inmates to take away the burned corpse.

Now, as I was overtaken by spasms, I rolled to the side of the road and fell into the ditch, coming dangerously close to the wires. My friends started screaming at the top of their lungs, "Mendel, straighten up! Don't touch the wires! Straighten up!"

I had no control over my body, but fortunately, after a minute or so, the spasms subsided. Slowly and carefully, I crawled back onto the road, relieved to have remained alive and hopeful that the Germans in the watchtowers hadn't seen me.

Despite the constant hunger and trauma, the desire for survival burned strong in my heart. Each time there was a *selektzia*, I was filled with terror and prayed to be kept alive a little longer. However, as our numbers kept dwindling, the fear kept growing that I would not be lucky forever.

At the end of Elul, as the *yomim tovim* approached, there were rumors in the camp that the Nazis liked to help the Jews "celebrate" by conducting *selektzias* during holidays. People worried if this pattern would repeat itself.

Our worst fears came true when, on September 17, Erev Rosh Hashanah, there was a *blocksperre*. Though I was in *block* 23 or 25, we were able to look down to the *shreib-shtube*, the office, which was situated in *Block 1*. To our dismay, we spotted Mengele's bicycle, which had a distinctive red wheel, parked next to the office. We knew that if Mengele was in the *lager*, another *selektzia* was in store.

While we waited for further orders, we sat together on the ground at the *appel platz*, reminiscing about Rosh Hashanah at home. The weather outside was beautiful, and we tried to forget the current danger as we discussed what special foods our families ate on Rosh Hashanah.

As we were talking, we suddenly heard a cantor singing "*Hinneni he'uni m'maas.*" The song was coming from the last *block* of inmates, *Block 27,* which was called the *revier.* When the *blockalteste* would see someone who couldn't walk on his feet anymore or was very sick, he would send him there. It was somewhat of an infirmary, and each time there was a *selektzia,* inmates from this *block* were sent to the gas chambers together with the inmates who had been pulled out.

(There was one more *block* on our side, *Block 29,* but that was the wash up *block,* not barracks used to house prisoners. There were several slop sinks inside, where inmates were taken in groups of ten to wash up. Additionally, when inmates died, their bodies were placed under these sinks. Each day, members of the *Toitens-Kommando* would go around the camp with wheelbarrows to collect the corpses from the barracks and stack them under the sinks in *Block 29.* Later, they were retrieved by other workers who transported the dead bodies to the crematoriums.)

As we listened to the cantor, we were electrified by the haunting melody and the singer's beautiful voice. We inched closer to the edge of the *appel platz,* trying to hear every word. In Vizhnitz, the *chazzan* says this *tefillah* quietly, so I had never heard this song before, but the soulful singing touched me deeply.

Suddenly, the singing stopped, and we were ordered to line up outside, in the yard between the barracks. One row had to step forward at a time, and Mengele inspected the people in that row. Those who passed inspection were ordered back inside the barracks, while the others had to wait on the road that ran between the two lines of barracks.

When Mengele approached my row, I screamed silently to myself, "*Zei mich nisht! Zei mich nisht! Zei mich nisht!*" ("Don't see me!") These words echoed loudly in my brain until Mengele passed my row. I would stand before him in three or four later inspections, and each time, this desperate cry reverberated within me.

I sighed with relief when Mengele finally passed me, but many weak and sick people were not as fortunate. They were sent out of the line and marched off together to one or two barracks that were then sealed shut.

There was one man whose young son of fourteen or fifteen was among those who were locked up. In the afternoon, after the *block-sperre*, the man began running around the *block* like a lion in a cage. He kept going next to the barracks and yelling for his son to stay in one corner and afterwards running elsewhere as he tried to figure out how to save his son. At one point, he began pulling at the sealed door and managed to rip the hinges partially off the wall. A small gap formed, and the boy, who was rather small, was able to sneak out. Soon, others inside enlarged the hole a bit and also squeezed through and escaped. Eventually, the *blockalteste* realized what was happening and put a stop to it. By then, ten or twenty people had slipped out, and he had to report the incident to the office.

The following morning, on the first day of Rosh Hashanah, a man began leading the Rosh Hashana *tefillos* in the *appel-platz* between *Block 21* and *23*, or perhaps it was between *Blocks 23* and *25*. This was the yard between the neighboring barracks, where the *appel* took place and food was distributed.

So many people were gathered there that I couldn't see who was *davening* or if he had a *machzer*. I was just eager to join the crowd and *daven* with everyone else. In hindsight, it's incredible to think how, even in that forsaken place, we did not forget *yom tov* and still remembered our Creator.

Several hours later, Mengele returned for another *selektzia*. Usually he wore gloves and appeared very composed. Now, he was not dressed as neatly as always and was clearly agitated. It was obvious that he was very angry because of the chaos and escapes.

The inmates of every two barracks were ordered to line up in the yard between their barracks. As we stood there, five men in each row, Mengele inspected each row, pointed at anyone who appeared shorter or weaker than the rest, and yelled, "Out! Out!" The guards stood ready beside him and immediately pulled out whomever he had pointed to.

When it became clear how this *selektzia* would work, the older people tried to take care of us young boys. They helped us stand on stones or told us to step on their feet to be taller. Indeed, this is how I was saved. Two older Jewish men stood on either side of me and instructed me to step onto their shoes. I stood like that until Mengele passed and managed to escape his attention. I don't know whether those men were Polish, Russian, or Hungarian, but they were Jewish men who held me up and saved my life.

As Mengele passed each row, he called *"Fartreiten!"* This was our command to step forward as he moved on to the next row. When we received that order, I stepped off the men's feet, took a step forward, and breathed a sigh of relief. I had managed to survive another day.

By the end of the *selektzia*, three or four entire *blocks* were filled with people. That night, on the second night of Rosh Hashana, there was another *blocksperre*. As we were locked inside our barracks, we heard a big commotion outside. Trucks or buses were going in and out, and we also heard the sound of sticks or wood breaking. When we came out the next morning, we found that all the sealed barracks had been completely emptied. All the occupants had been taken to feed the ever hungry crematoriums.

Of course, those barracks did not stay empty for long. Very soon, they were filled once again with more newcomers to Birkenau. Meanwhile, we had a bit of a reprieve, as we did not see Mengele again for a few days.

Our *blockalteste* at the time was a Polish fellow who was about twenty-five or twenty-six years old and training to be a priest. He was a very fine person and tried to make things easier for us when he could. On Erev Yom Kippur, he tried to help us prepare by arranging for us to eat before sundown.

Typically, the kitchen in *Block 1* would start distributing the food at around twelve noon. Whoever had been selected to bring the food

that day would carry it back to the field next to our *block*. Food distribution was a lengthy ordeal, since it took time for everyone to line up
and receive their allotment of food. Usually the drums were ready to
be sent back to the kitchen at around four or five in the afternoon, but
sometimes, when inmates arrived at the kitchen late, they had to wait a
long time for their food and distribution lasted until ten o'clock.

"Today I'll make sure to send you for food as early as possible," the
blockaltste told us.

Early in the morning he sent down the *shtube-dinst* with a list of
how many people were in the *block*, so the kitchen workers could prepare our food. Since the number of people varied, this count was sent
daily to the kitchen so that they would know how many drums to prepare for each *block*.

Despite his efforts, we did not receive our food until evening. The
Germans knew that Yom Kippur fell that night, and they deliberately
started the food distribution only at five or six o'clock. As a result, the
drums arrived too late and we didn't eat that day.

The next morning, the *blockalteste* said, "Today, I'll send for food
as late as possible. If we'll be one of the last to receive our drums, it
won't get here until four or five in the afternoon. You should be able to
eat after nightfall."

Once again, however, the devious Nazis foiled his plans. That day,
they sounded the alarm at eleven in the morning, ordering everyone
to line up and send for food. This was earlier than usual to ensure that
the Jews who were fasting on Yom Kippur would not have a chance to
eat that day after the fast ended.

Whenever food was distributed, we were first given bowls that
were then filled with soup. The only thing we kept was our spoons. The
bowls had to be returned each day, making it impossible for anyone to
save their food for later. Somehow, though, I was able to find a shallow
dish that had a handle attached to it. I poured the red cabbage soup I
received into it and returned my bowl with everyone else. I held the

handle and carried the soup around with me, hoping to save it until nightfall when I would be able to eat.

All of a sudden, there were orders for a *blocksperre*. We soon learned that Mengele was in our *lager*. The adults began urging us young kids to eat whatever food we had saved so that we would pass inspection. "You must eat! You must eat!" they insisted.

Realizing that this was a matter of *pekuach nefesh*, I ate the soup I had been carrying around. The grown -ups then began pinching our cheeks, trying to get some color in our faces.

At around two or three in the afternoon, we were taken to the *shports-platz*, a sports field that had goal towers at the two ends and was meant to be used for playing soccer. We were told that some people would be taken to Germany to pick potatoes and that they were specifically looking for young kids, who could bend down and pick them up easily.

An assistant was ordered to bring a stick with nails. We were terrified and first thought that this would be knocked into someone. Instead, Mengele picked out one young boy and made him stand in front of the goal post. Then he ordered the assistant to knock the stick into the post, right above the boy's head, so that it now looked like an inverted L.

Mengele now turned his attention back to the crowd. He ordered all of us to pass in front of the goal post in single file. Anyone who did not reach the stick would have to go to the left side; anyone taller would go to the right.

An SS officer stood at the goal post observing the people as they passed by. Despite his presence, the stick, which had only been knocked in with a single nail, did not stay stationary throughout the *selektzia*. The crowd was too large, and there were many distractions as people were sent to thc left or right. As a result, some men succeeded in secretly pushing the stick down as they passed.

To my good fortune, a tall person passed right before me and he managed to push down the stick a bit. Thus, I was slightly taller than the stick when I walked passed it and was not pulled out to go to the left side.

At some point during the *selektzia*, some young boys who had been sent to the left managed to sneak into the larger group of taller men. When other boys realized that they hadn't been caught, they attempted to do the same. Suddenly, there was a large commotion, with guards yelling and boys running. Mengele became very angry. He ordered all those that had been sent to the right to take their shirts off and walk in front of him for a second *selektzia*. Eventually, the *selektzia* was halted and all who had been sent to the left were locked up in two barracks.[11]

Tragically, most boys who had been part of my original group did not survive the Rosh Hashana and Yom Kippur *selektzias*. Some of them had already perished earlier, but of those who were left, most were picked out. In fact, of the 900 young teens who had been together with me since Shavuous, only about twenty were left. (Of these twenty, I know five who survived.) I had come dangerously close to being sent off to the crematoriums and I realized that I would not be so fortunate the next time.

The day after Yom Kippur, many men tried to join work groups that were being formed to leave camp for other sub-camps and work

---

11   The account of this Yom Kippur *selektzia* was corroborated by Yoseph Zalman Kleinman, a witness at the Eichman trial in Israel. Years later, I also heard it from another survivor during a *shiva* visit to my daughter-in-law Naomi's uncle, Mendel Gottlieb. Mendel had lost his sister and was sitting *shiva* together with his brother-in-law, Yosef Muller. While I was there, he asked where I had been during the war. We quickly realized that we had both been at this *selektzia* (though he had remained in Birkenau and was liberated there).

While we recalled the terrible events of that day, the *rav* and several board members of Muller's shul on Long Island were also present. They later admitted that they had heard the story from him many times but assumed that it had been embellished as time passed and memory faded. Only now, after hearing it from me too, did they realize that every detail was true.

Every Rosh Hashana and Yom Kippur, during the *tefillah* of *U'nesana Tokef*, I think of this day as I say the words "*k'vakoras roeh edro.*" I remember this goal post *selektzia* and thank Hashem that I survived that *gehinom*.

sites. In the past, they had tried to avoid going on *kommandos* because they were afraid of the deadly coal mines and hard labor. However, with so many *selektzias* taking place, the *kommandos* suddenly seemed to be the lesser of the two evils.

Until now, I always stood aside and watched as newly-formed *kommandos* were led out of the camp. Now, I realized that this might indeed be the only way to survive. If the Nazis decided to celebrate Sukkos with another *selektzia*, chances were slim that I would survive it.

It was time for me to try to get out of Birkenau too.

CHAPTER SEVEN: THE WINTER OF DESPAIR

I t was already late in the afternoon when I resolved to join a *kommando* to get out of the camp. Now, my mind was racing as I tried to figure out how to implement my plan.

As I was standing next to the barracks, I saw some commotion in the lower *blocks* on the other side of the road. While we were able to speak with inmates in the *blocks* beside ours, we were not permitted to cross the wide marching road in the center of the *lager* and go to the barracks opposite ours.

I watched the action from across the road and realized that another *kommando* was being organized. I knew that this was my chance for survival. *I cannot survive another selektzia*, I thought to myself. *There is no one smaller left in the camp. If I want to survive, I must take action now.*

Mustering all my courage, I called out to the few friends I had left. "I'm taking a chance and running across!"

Another boy, Meisels, agreed to join me, and together we ran across the road and quickly mingled with the men who were on the other side. We soon learned that a group of one hundred men was being formed, and it seemed that carpenters were among the people who were chosen. I figured that if I had to be a carpenter to survive, I'd be a carpenter.

As I stood at the end of the line with my friend, the sun was beginning to set. At last, the two of us were standing in front of the *meister*. "What do you do?" he asked. Relying on the information I'd heard, I replied, "I'm a *tischler*."

"What kind of *tischler* are you?" the man asked.

I stood there quietly, not knowing how to respond. What kind of carpenter? I hadn't realized I'd need more information about my new profession.

Fortunately, a German soldier who stood beside the *meister* became impatient. "So? A *mabel tischler* or a building *tischler*?" he asked.

Thinking quickly, I reasoned that a furniture carpenter probably did more intricate work than a building carpenter. How hard could it be to learn how to build? "Building!" I replied.

Next, they turned to my friend and asked his profession.

"I'm a glazier," Meisels replied. His father dealt in glass and mirrors, so he was somewhat familiar with the work involved.

We were both pushed toward the group of people that had been chosen for the new *kommando*. By then, they had almost 100 men, and we were one of the last few to join the group.

Once the group was complete, we were all taken to be tattooed. We would no longer be living in limbo at Birkenau, waiting to survive another *selektzia*. We would be joining the Nazis' slave labor work force and would need a unique identification number.

We were ordered to line up to have our identification number tattooed on our left arm. When I reached the front of the line, blue ink was smeared on my skin. Then, using a needle, a man formed a letter and a series of numbers with quick, successive pricks. The process wasn't very painful; I felt like I was simply being pinched. The number I was given—and that I still carry today—was B10573. From that day on, I had to identify myself to camp authorities as "B, *hindret finef un drei-in-zibitzig*."[12]

---

12   Some years ago, when I was in Florida, I met a developer, a Chassidishe *yid* from Toronto.

Once we had all been tattooed, our group was taken to trucks and driven to the main administration office of Auschwitz. There, we heard the *meister* bargaining with office staff. The Nazis wanted ten *Reichsmark* per head, but he wanted to pay only five. After some back and forth, they agreed on six *Reichsmark* per head.

Thus, one day after Yom Kippur, on September 28, 1944, I was sold together with a group of men to the German *meister* of Gleiwitz for six *Reichsmark*. I had just turned fifteen.

As night fell, we were surrounded by a group of German guards. They traveled with us for more than an hour. After ten o'clock that night, we arrived in Gleiwitz Tzvei, an industrial labor camp that had opened in May of 1944 and was one of the sub-camps of Auschwitz.[13]

After we arrived in Gleiwitz, we were given very hot showers and new striped uniforms consisting of pants, jackets, and striped caps. We received a new insignia, a star consisting of a yellow triangle that pointed up and a red triangle that pointed down. The yellow star was the standard symbol of Jewish prisoners, while red inverted triangles were usually used for political prisoners. For some reason, in Gleiwitz, this was the star that everyone received.[14]

There were between 1,000 and 1,100 workers in Gleiwitz. Over 300 women worked in the production of coal tar, while the majority, some 700 men, repaired and maintained factory machinery and

---

When we exchanged war experiences, we realized that we had both been in Birkenau. The man turned out to be Meisels, and indeed, when we rolled up our sleeves, we discovered that his number was only one after mine!

13   There were four Gleiwitz camps in all. Gleiwitz I opened in March 1944 and had over 1,300 prisoners who worked on railroad repair. Gleiwitz III opened in July and had between 500 and 600 prisoners, who worked mostly on production of weapons, ammunition, and railway wheels. Gleiwitz IV opened in June and had only a little over 400 workers, who repaired military vehicles and expanded barracks, often working in airports or on roads. All the Gleiwitz camps closed on January 17 or 18 of 1945.

14   Political prisoners, most of whom were Polish citizens, were often referred to as "*roite vinkel*" because of the red inverted triangle on their prison uniforms. Common German criminals wore a green inverted triangle and were known as "*grine vinkel*." Therefore, our Gleiwitz stars, which were different from the typical yellow stars worn by Jewish inmates, identified us as Jewish political prisoners.

helped with the expansion of the factory. A barbed wire separated the men's and women's sections of the camp and only *kapos*—inmates in charge of work teams—could go back and forth through the door that separated the two parts.

The new arrivals were spread among the five men's barracks in the camp. As soon as I walked into the *block*, I realized that I was in a relatively good camp. There was a piece of bread and margarine on the beds next to some people, an astonishing sight for us new arrivals. I would later learn, that in this camp inmates received sixty dekagrams, or twenty-one ounces, of bread—either three ends or one long piece of bread.

The *unter-Kapo* at Gleiwitz was a very nice man whose name was Munchno. He was a Jewish fellow, a big, tall guy from Warsaw. As soon as we arrived, he made an appeal, going around the camp and asking for people to give some food for the *muselmen*[15] from Birkenau.

Munchno went even a step further. He spoke to the few hundred people who worked for a German company making light coal. When they returned from work, they were as black as chimney cleaners from all the dust, and they showered daily to clean up. These men received sweet farina once or twice each week, and somehow, Munchno convinced them to give this extra food to us for nourishment the next few times they received it. It was quite dangerous to organize a redistribution of food in this manner, but Munchno clearly felt bad for us newcomers and went out of his way to help us.

The next morning, the new arrivals were ordered to line up. As we stood there to be counted, we appeared to be the biggest *kommando* in the camp. We were all served black coffee, and afterwards, we were told that we would be taken to a worksite outside the camp.

We walked across an open field for one or two kilometers, near the coal mines that were being built close to the factory. Once we were

---

15   *Muselmann* literally means "Muslim." Somehow, this word came to refer to skeletal, emaciated inmates or those too weak to work.

in the field, we were again asked what our occupations were. Again I said that I am a *tischler*. The overseer had nothing for me to do, and together with some other twenty people or so, I was assigned to move rocks back and forth from one side of the field to the other.

When we returned to camp, we were counted again and then served the biggest meal we had received in a long time: soup, a big piece of bread—like we had seen some inmates hold the previous night—and marmalade. Indeed, this was the standard dinner in that camp, though the marmalade was sometimes replaced with margarine.

For the next day or two, I was again given meaningless, difficult tasks. Afterwards, we were finally assigned to more productive, albeit backbreaking, work. We were ordered to help dig a canal, which was being built along the side of the road for large pipes. The ditch was quite deep and we had to dig through sticky, yellow mud, forming this canal by hand.

The work was divided between several groups of people. Workers from the lowest platform threw up mud with a shovel to the second platform. From there, workers threw the mud up to a third group that was standing on the street with little wagons to take the mud away. More often than not, mud fell down on the first group of workers as it was being transferred from the second platform to the road. I had the misfortune to be assigned to the lowest platform, and when I came out after a day of work, I was covered with yellow mud. We were quite a sight and had to wash up when we returned to camp.

Our *fuhr-arbeiter*, or foreman, was named Szukaft. He was a skinny little fellow who was generally a nice person, but in the field, he gave us a tough time. When we returned the first night, the *unter-Kapo*, Muncho, asked us how Szukaft had treated us. People responded honestly, saying that he had been very mean and was yelling at us the entire time. Hearing this, Muncho grabbed Szukaft by the collar and lifted him into the air. "If you touch these *muselmen*," he warned, "if you do anything to them, don't bother coming back to camp. I'll choke you! I'll kill you!"

Poor Szukaft started crying like a little child. "German soldiers were standing nearby. I had to scream to show that everyone was working hard. Please, I didn't do anything. I couldn't have them see anyone shirking their work!"

"Why don't you give them a signal?" Muncho asked. "Like this you can warn them if the Germans are approaching and they'll make sure to work really hard then."

Szukaft agreed immediately to this idea since he had not meant to make life more difficult for us. He told us that if the Germans were approaching, he would yell, "Six!" If they were almost at the ditch, he would yell, "Double six!"

It was a good arrangement and worked well for several weeks. After that, our assignment at the ditches was suddenly over. Either the work had been completed to the Germans' satisfaction or it had simply become too cold to dig through the ground.

Next, we were assigned to cement work. There were big, heavy bags that were filled with cement, perhaps as much as fifty pounds of it. We had to unload them very quickly. Sometimes we had to load the cement into a mixer, and other times we formed pipes with it. It was also very dirty and sticky work. Every few days, we were reassigned to different cement work.

In Gleiwitz there were several hundred British prisoners-of-war, as well as some civil workers, who lived in town. The soldiers fared relatively well, since they received Red Cross packages every week or two. We were able to barter for items with these two groups, and sometimes, when there were large deliveries, the soldiers gave us entire care packages.

These British soldiers sometimes made life quite interesting at camp. They were guarded by older men who carried huge guns that were almost as big as they were. Often, as they went to their work site, the soldiers started walking very quickly and the guards had to run to catch up with them. "Not so fast! Not so fast!" they'd scream. Of course, this was quite comical to watch and we felt fantastic when we saw how frustrated the guards became.

The care packages the soldiers received often had cigarettes, a highly desirable item in the camp. Once, a guard asked one of the prisoners for the cigarette he was smoking. "I'll give you half of it," the man replied.

He handed half the cigarette to the guard and then put the second half on the ground and pushed it into the mud with his heel. He wanted to tease the guard and show him that he'd rather waste the cigarette than let him enjoy it.

Of course, we took great pleasure from the soldiers' antics. Years later, when I watched episodes from Hogan's Heroes, it seemed to me that some of the Gleiwitz incidents had inspired events in the series.

As autumn gave way to winter, the weather at Gleiwitz became brutally cold. The work assignments also changed, and we began assisting with the production of soft coal, called coke, which was used to make synthetic rubber. Our task was to stand beside narrow tracks, which carried small railroad lorries that were filled with coal. We had to pull a plug and tilt these lorries to empty them. Afterwards, a few people had to work together to lift the heavy lorries off the narrow tracks. It was miserable work. If one person was shorter than the others, he had to carry the entire weight of the lorry on his own.

Since it was so cold outside, we were sometimes allowed to take short breaks to warm up next to barrels of coke. Sometimes we also huddled close to the factory walls. There were big stoves inside with fires that burned all day to process the coal. We could feel the warmth even on the outside of the walls and tried warming ourselves there.

At one point during that difficult winter, I became sick. Throughout the war, whenever I felt my chances of survival were slim, I'd tell myself, "I want to live just one hour in Palestine and after that, I don't care what happens to me." In Birkenau, I'd refused to believe that the "only way out is through the chimney," and now, I could still not accept that I would be burned or thrown to the dogs like other unfortunate inmates. I was only fourteen or fifteen, but for me, the most important thing during my time in Birkenau, Gleiwitz, and later in other camps, was to survive long enough so that I would be buried with dignity.

There was a *blockalteste* in Gleiwitz whose name, if I recall correctly, was Avrum Applebaum. He was a Polish Jew, a very fine person. Seeing how weak I was, he allowed my friends and me to take pieces of potatoes and put them on the stove. We hoped to turn them into edible potato pieces, something resembling potato chips.

This *blockalteste* would have been shot had someone caught us, but he bravely stood watch by the window, allowing us to prepare the potatoes. He was a wonderful person who tried to help whomever he could. I don't know whether he survived the war, but he is someone who deserves credit for making our lives easier.

Gleiwitz was a camp that provided good food, but the work was brutal. Whether we thought this was a fair exchange or not hardly mattered. Soon enough, we learned that we wouldn't be staying at the camp much longer.

Around January 15, one of the Nazis gave a speech, informing us that we would soon receive instructions to evacuate the camp, since the Russian front was approaching. Indeed, a day or two later, we were awakened in the middle of the night. The *lager-alteste*, the highest ranking prisoner, went around to wake everyone up. "*Antreiten!* We're moving out!" came the command.

The area where the clothing was stored was opened up and everyone was instructed to put on as many layers of clothing as they could. Each person also took an extra shirt to tie into a rucksack. We received five loaves of bread and some margarine, with a warning that there would be no more distribution of food. We stored the bread inside our makeshift sacks. By nine o'clock in the morning, we began moving out.

We left the camp and marched for eighteen hours continuously. Every once in a while a motorcycle with a Nazi officer approached to give orders to the soldiers who were guarding us. Late at night, we finally stopped in a barn of hay and slept for a few hours. When we woke up, we received no additional food and continued marching in the bitter cold.

A short while after we started walking, we met another group that was coming back from the camp we were heading towards. Apparently, too many groups had arrived there and they could no longer accommodate new arrivals.

We were instructed to turn back. We kept walking, though this time we took another, much shorter route. It seems that we had deliberately been taken on a circuitous route the day before. After a few hours, we arrived in the town of Gleiwitz, which was located near our camp and had given it its name. We were taken to a big plaza in the center of town, which was surrounded by large two- or three-family houses.

When we arrived, it was midday, on Sunday, January 20. Many people were passing by, coming from or going to church or taking care of errands. Some of them threw objects at us or spit at us as they passed. Others stared straight ahead, pretending that they didn't see us at all.

As we stood there, I suddenly spotted a dirty white dog carrying a bone in its mouth across the plaza. As I watched the dog, I thought, *I wish I can turn into this dog so that I too can eat a bone and roam around freely!*

We didn't quite understand why we had been taken to the center of town. Was it simply to make a spectacle of ourselves, have people spit at us and degrade us? There seemed to be no real purpose, since after a few hours, we were taken to the town's train station.

When we arrived at the train station, we found many railroad cars that were being filled with arrivals from many local camps, all sub-camps of Auschwitz. With clubs in their hands and bloodcurdling screams, SS officers chased us into the remaining cars until there was no room to put in a pin.

These cars weren't cattle cars, like we had ridden before, but open railroad cars. After every two cars there was a place on the outside for a brake man to stand, and now the SS took their positions there. They were carrying guns in their hands and warned us that anyone caught jumping from the train would be shot. No food or water was distributed at all. Finally, as night began to fall, the train started moving.

For days, we rode on that train, passing towns in Poland and Slovakia. We were terribly cold and very crowded. We could hardly breathe due to the overcrowding. We were packed so tightly together, body to body, that even though we were starving, we could not bend down to reach for the food that remained in the sacks at our feet. Anyone who tried to do so risked being smothered by the crowd.

As day after day passed, many on the train perished. I remember a father with four or five sons from Absha. They died within four or five days and were thrown out from the car. Since the SS shot at anyone or anything that was thrown over the train cars, passengers waited until after dark to throw out the bodies of the dead. Another family I remember was a father with two teenage boys, about fourteen and seventeen. The three of them spoke Czech, and at one point, we passed an area near their hometown that the father recognized. He told the boys to jump off and gave them instructions to run and hide in a specific home nearby. "Don't look back for your brother," the father told them. "When you hit the ground, just run!" The older boy followed his father's instructions and jumped out. The younger one was afraid and hesitated, so the father pushed him off the train. Fortunately, there were no shots, but I don't know if the brothers survived.

As soon as there was a little room on the trains, a couple of big shots demanded extra space to sit on the floor. As more people died, there was more room in the cars for the rest of us too. Although we could now reach the sacks at our feet, the bread had long become soggy and disintegrated and was no longer edible.

We did not receive additional food, but we did manage to get some water. Someone attached a pail or cup to the end of a string, and as the train traveled, it collected some snow. Usually, however, everyone grabbed the cup whenever it was pulled back and hardly anyone received anything.

As we traveled, it kept snowing intermittently. Each time the snow fell, people tried to lick the snow off each other. Some people actually went out of their minds. They began fighting with their neighbors, yelling, "If you don't let me lick you off, you can't lick me off either!"

At some point, I turned to my neighbor and said, "What are we doing here? Let's get off the train!"

Like many others on the train, the hunger, thirst, and congestion was causing me to have hallucinations. My neighbor tried bringing me back to my senses and yelled, "Mendel! Mendel! Wake up!"

One day we stopped near some locomotives at a station in Slovakia. We motioned with our hands and Slovakian conductors brought us buckets of water. There was a lumber camp at that location, and people started making snowballs and throwing them to us so that we could drink. When the Germans realized what was happening, they began shooting into the air and warned everyone to stop.

Our train was moved to the side tracks, perhaps to clean the tracks. We saw an overpass that was situated just in front of us. We could see that it was filled with people, and we assumed that they had come to jeer at the dying Jews. However, once the train started moving and it went under the overpass, the people began throwing down raw potatoes, bread, and clothes. We tried grabbing whatever we could. This happened several times during the trip that Czechoslovakian peasants took pity on us and tried to throw things into the wagons.

The train kept moving, until at last, more than ten days after we'd left Gleiwitz, we arrived in Oranienburg, a town about thirty-five kilometers (almost twenty-two miles) from Berlin, Germany.

Throughout this long trip, as well as during other travels by train or marches by foot between camps, I never felt the need to relieve my-self. There were no buckets provided on the train for this purpose, and as far as I remember, no one needed them. This was the result of the trauma and stress of our situation, as well as our general malnourish-ment and the lack of meals during the trip. Our normal bodily func-tions returned once we were settled in a new camp and some routine had been restored, together with regular meals, however paltry they may have been.

After we pulled into the station in Oranienburg and the railroad cars were opened, most of us could hardly walk. We stumbled out, about sixty or seventy men from each car, many of them very sick. When we departed from Gleiwitz, there had been about 170 or 180 inmates per car. Clearly, the Nazis didn't always need gas chambers to carry out their Final Solution. They had managed to reduce our num-bers by almost two-thirds simply by giving us an extended train ride, sans food and water, of course.

The date was around January 30. I wondered how much longer I could survive.

CHAPTER EIGHT:
THE NIGHTMARE CONTINUES

Oranienburg served as a *zamelpunkt*, a place where inmates came from surrounding areas and were then sent further to other camps. Additionally, Sachsenhausen-Oranienburg,[16] as the camp is often called, had long-term "residents" who belonged to its own forced labor units. Among the most infamous ongoing operations at the camp was one of the largest currency counterfeiting operations ever recorded. The Germans forced imprisoned artists to produce forged British and American currency, as well as official documents like passports, as part of a plan to undermine the financial stability of these countries.

When our transport first arrived in Oranienburg, we saw large

---

16 Sachsenhausen-Oranienburg opened in July of 1936. Initially, there was only a small number of Jews there, as the camp held mostly political prisoners and "asocials," cripples, beggars, alcoholics, criminals, homosexuals, Roma and Sinti (Gypsies), and others who the Nazis believed did not belong in their superior society. One exception was a brief period following *Kristallnacht* when almost 6,000 Jews were sent to Oranienburg. Most were released in the ensuing months, often in exchange for stated intent to emigrate. During the last year of the war, large transports of Jews began arriving in the camp. By the beginning of 1945, there were over 11,000 Jews in the camp.

Some 200,000 people passed through the camp between 1936 and 1945. About 40,000 or 50,000 died from exhaustion, malnutrition, disease, executions, and experiments. (In 1941, at least 12,000 were killed during the testing of gassing vehicles and other execution methods.) Most of the inmates who were killed were Russian prisoners of war, among them many Jews. Later, many more died when 33,000 prisoners were taken on a forced death march in the final weeks of the war. (Sources: United States Holocaust Memorial Museum and Sachsenhausen Memorial and Museum) vats that were filled with green water stationed around the camp. We were desperately thirsty, but we were warned by prisoners that the water was poisoned. The vats were kept there as a safety measure, to battle flames in case the camp suffered a direct hit from American bombs. The poison was supposed to keep parched inmates like us from drinking the water.

Despite the warnings, several men were so thirsty that they could not think rationally or resist the temptation to drink the water. They ran to the vats and grabbed a few handfuls to drink. Almost instantly, they started having convulsions and died.

On our first night in Oranienburg, we finally received some warm tea. Afterwards, we were led into a structure that looked like a large airplane hangar and went to sleep there.

As soon as it became light outside, we were chased out of the hangar. We received some black coffee early in the morning. Afterwards, we remained outside until lunchtime, when we were finally served some food again.

The food distribution at Oranienburg was very inefficient. There were only three doors from which five or six thousand prisoners were served. As such, it took several hours for everyone to receive food, and some people were trampled to death during the desperate stampede for food. This happened three times each day.

One of the unusual sights in Oranienburg was that of a group of inmates constantly marching around the perimeter of the large *appelplatz*. The men kept going back and forth, sometimes singing as they marched under the careful watch of the Germans. Some of the unfortunate men recruited for this operation would fall dead each day during the relentless march. I heard from some of the other men that the Germans were trying to see how long their soldiers could march continuously at the front lines without succumbing to exhaustion.[17]

---

17   According to post-war accounts, prisoners in Oranienbrug covered between sixteen and
      twenty-five miles each day as they marched around the perimeter of the roll call area. The

After about eight days in Oranienburg, we were once again put onto railroad cars. During this trip to a worker's camp, the Germans gave one kilo of bread for every three people, as well as a piece of very salty cheese. We received no water at all. On the second day of our trip, we received the same food again, but we could not eat the salty cheese because we were so thirsty.

After traveling for two days, we arrived at our next destination: Flossenbürg.[18] The camp was situated in Bavaria, Germany, near the border with Czechoslovakia. We arrived before nightfall, probably around February 10.

Fortunately, we didn't lose any inmates during this relatively short trip. Nonetheless, while we were all alive, we were desperately thirsty and very weak. The station was about two miles from the camp. Though we could barely stand, we had to march in orderly rows under the strict watch of the SS guards.

Since the camp was situated on a hill, we walked uphill from the train station to the camp. On both sides of the road, narrow streams of dirty water carried away melted ice and snow. Some of us began drinking this dirty water, but the guards beat anyone they caught drinking.

After we arrived in Flossenbürg, we were counted and taken to barracks that were surrounded by ankle-deep mud. These *blocks* were

---

purpose of these marches was to test military footwear for the Germans.

Additionally, there have been allegations that an experimental drug was given to inmates at Oranienburg towards the end of the war. The drug was designed to increase stamina and endurance for German soldiers. It is possible that some of the forced daily marches were designed to test this new drug during its development.

18   The first prisoners arrived in Flossenbürg in May of 1938. By February 1943, there were over 4,000 prisoners: Soviet, Polish, Czech, Dutch, and German political prisoners, as well as German criminals and other "asocials."

From August 1944 through March 1945, at least 23,000 Jews arrived from evacuated camps in the neighboring regions. By March 1945, there were 53,000 prisoners in the Flossenbürg camp system, with 14,500 in the main camp and the rest in surrounding sub-camps.

Nearly 97,000 prisoners, including 16,000 women, passed through the Flossenbürg system in all. An estimated 30,000 prisoners, including 3,515 Jews, died in Flossenbürg and its sub-camps or on the evacuation route.

(Source: United States Holocaust Memorial Museum)

in a quarantine area, separated from the rest of the camp by a wire fence—not electric but regular wire—and it was here that new arrivals were processed before joining the other inmates.

On the first or second day after our arrival, we were taken to the showers. We had to take off all our clothes and leave them behind. The showers contained disinfectant, leaving us with the same terrible smell and oily feel of that first shower in Birkenau. Afterwards we received thin, new clothes that could not possibly protect us from the cold. Everyone received a jacket and pants; some lucky ones received underpants too. No one received socks or hats.

It was still bitterly cold, but there was no way to get back the warmer clothes we had worn upon our arrival. So, a few days after our showers, some men began "organizing" for warm things to wear. When the *blockalteste* realized this, he made an inspection and beat anyone caught with an extra item of clothing.

Flossenbürg was a camp that was unusually corrupt, and many vicious people held positions of power. In addition to the SS officers, there were unarmed Ukrainians guards who could be identified by their black uniforms. They were often more vicious than the Nazis and abused the inmates mercilessly. Additionally, since the camp had originally housed only political and criminal prisoners, these old-timers had moved up in rank. Many murderers and convicts were now *blockaltestes* who took pleasure in torturing the inmates in their charge.

Indeed, our *blockateste* was one such fellow. He chased us out of our barrack at five thirty in the morning, and we had to stand outside in the cold for thirty minutes or an hour until we received our morning coffee. Afterwards we went back inside for a short while and were then sent out again at eight, when the barracks were cleaned.

Since it was so cold outside, we sometimes hid in the latrine or tried to press ourselves under a roof at the side of the barrack. However, wherever we went to find shelter, the *blockalteste* would find us and chase us away.

An hour before lunch, we were already ordered to line up outside, always in the area that had the deepest mud. When everyone's feet were soaked and partially frozen, we were finally served some soup. We seldom received a complete portion, as the food was served quickly and carelessly.

Between six and seven in the evening, we were chased out for another *appel*. After we were all counted, we received our evening bread.

During this period, I met several young boys, who had all come on my transport to Flossenbürg. From Ruscova (the town where I'd picked up meat from my cousin), there were Leiby Hecht, his cousins, two Hecht brothers, and Baruch Feig. There was a short boy whom we called Moishele from Klausenberg, and from Oyber-Visheve there were Yossi Yankovitch and myself. Once we realized that we were all young teens from the same area, we stuck together and tried to help each other.

After several days, our group was moved from the quarantine barracks. Most of the labor at Flossenbürg involved the production of aircraft parts, and we were assigned to one of such *kommandos*. Our group was number *tzvunzieg-nul-fier* (2004), and our job was to carry large metal rods, about one-and-a-half inches by sixteen feet in size, together with a partner. However, soon afterwards, I was taken out together with the other teens to the *jugent-block*, the youth barrack that held all the inmates under the age of eighteen.

My friends and I were among 120 to 140 Jewish boys who were in the youth barrack. The rest were Russian and Ukrainian teens, who were determined to make our lives miserable. When food was distributed, for example, they grabbed our bread as soon as we walked into the *block* or took our marmalade out of our hands. Though we tried hiding our food under our shirts, they still sometimes managed to steal it.

After a few days, we complained to the *blockalteste*, a *grine vinkel*— a German murderer who had been from the camp's earlier inmates.

Instead of telling the other boys to stop stealing, he yelled, "You Jews can't live in civilized society without complaining!"

Across a big plaza were the *prominenten-blocks*, barracks that housed famous political prisoners. Among them were former members of the Hungarian government, including its leader, Miklós Horthy, and French Socialist leader Léon Blum. They received better treatment than other inmates, and we sometimes smuggled ourselves across to their barracks to hunt for food.

I remember one incident when I found one of the men about to spill water from a pot of cooked potatoes. I ran toward him with a bowl. The man looked at me and said, "You want the water? Sure, I can give you the water." I took this precious potato water back to share with my friends.

Another place where we could obtain food or other items was at our camp's thriving black market. Each day after work, prisoners were free to roam around the camp for half an hour. During that time, men would gather in the plaza to exchange bread or soup for other food, pants, socks, or the most coveted item, cigarettes. The Ukrainian guards would mingle with the prisoners, often making trades themselves. The Germans were probably aware of this daily bazaar but they did not interfere.

One day, some Russian kids from our barrack wanted to go organize some things at a time when we were not permitted to leave our barrack. They jumped out of a window to avoid detection and landed among some flowers. These flowers had been planted at our *appel-platz* and along the back of our *block* under the direction of our *blockalteste*. Now, as the boys jumped onto them, the flowers were trampled and ruined.

The *blockalteste* became enraged when he found the ruined flowers and naturally blamed the Jewish boys. "You *farfluchte Juden*!" he yelled. "You ruined my flowers! You were born to be locked up in a ghetto! From now on, you'll be in your own little ghetto here too!"

The man took some barbed wire and formed an enclosure around one row of beds. Each row held five beds of three layers each. In this mini ghetto, he squeezed about one hundred and twenty teens.

In Birkenau, the bunks were very wide and it was possible to squeeze six people on each side of the bed, for a total of twelve, sleeping head to foot alternatively. Here, the bunks were much narrower and they typically held only two men on each side, for a total of four per bunk. Now, in our cramped quarters, we tried to squeeze six or seven boys per bunk, but there still wasn't enough room for everyone. Many of us slept in partially sitting positions, and some had to sleep on the floor. If anyone moved too much, he would be cut by the wire attached to the bunks.

Another source of torment was the weekly *antloizen*, the inspections for lice in the camp. This took place each Shabbos evening, after the distribution of food.

The men in charge of lice inspection were vicious Russian men. The inmates had to take their shirts off and put them on inside out. Then, we walked past the inspectors in single file so that they could examine the seams of our shirts. The inspectors would take out anyone found with lice. At times, they simply chose not to check one of the Jewish inmates and send him to be deloused with the infested men.

All those found with lice were quarantined and taken away at ten o'clock at night. They were led to a room where they were ordered to strip and put their clothes in a big boiler to be washed and steamed. Next, they were given a shower, which had that oily, foul-smelling disinfectant added to the water. Afterwards, the men had to wait until five in the morning for their clothes to be ready. In the meantime, they remained there, wet and shivering in the cold night. When they grew tired, they lay down on the cold cement floor to rest.

When the clothes were finally returned at dawn, each man received a wet jacket and pair of pants that he had to put on immediately. The clothes were left to dry on the shivering inmates.

It is no surprise that many inmates grew sick from this delousing process. In fact, anyone picked out for *antloizen* two or three times was doomed to almost certain death from pneumonia.

That year, in 1945, Rosh Chodesh Nissan fell on March 15. The first night of Pesach fell on Wednesday, March 28. After Rosh Chodesh, my friends and I discussed how to prepare for Pesach. We knew it would be difficult to survive only on soup for a week and wondered how we could possibly avoid eating bread. We decided that each day one of us would exchange our bread for several potatoes at the market. By the time Pesach arrived, we would have enough potatoes to survive without eating any bread.

At first, things went as planned. Despite our hunger, we each took a turn to skip our daily bread and exchange it for potatoes. We "organized" strings to tie at the bottoms of our pants, around our ankles, so that we could store our potatoes inside our pants and keep them from falling out. It seemed the safest place to store food in the camp. Indeed, I managed to walk around with three potatoes around one leg and four around the other, with the strings keeping them safely in place. At that point we didn't know yet how we would cook the potatoes, but we decided to take one day at a time.

Only a few days before Pesach our plans were ruined by the vicious Russian lice inspectors in our *block*. During the weekly *antloizen*, they decided to send all the Jewish boys from our barracks for delousing. My friends and I had no choice but to undress when ordered and leave our clothes to be washed and steamed. Of course, inside our pants were the precious potatoes we had accumulated with such difficulty. It was heartbreaking to lose them only days before *yom tov*.

We spent the night without clothes, on the cold, cement floor. Finally, at around 4:30 in the morning, we all received newly-steamed clothes and were ordered to return to our *block*. To my dismay, I realized that my new pants were much lighter than the pair I'd been assigned previously, which had offered some protection from the cold.

In the weeks that followed, I had to save up a few portions of bread to organize new pants. Ultimately, I managed to procure a pair of French army pants shortly before I left the camp.

In the end, I think we survived mostly on soup that Pesach, exchanging our bread for an extra plate of soup.

About a week after Pesach, approximately April 10, there was a sudden order: "*Juden, arois!*" All Jews throughout the camp had to gather in one place. We were counted and held there for a while, but later we were sent back to our original barracks.

Several days passed and then, on about April 15, we were given the same order: "*Juden, arois!*" Once again, we lined up perfectly, and this time we were marched out of the camp. We walked for about two miles, heading back to the train station where we had arrived about two months earlier.

We Jews had arrived in Flossenbürg on an exclusively Jewish transport. True, in the camp we had been divided among the other inmates, but for our departure, we were organized into an exclusively Jewish transport once again.

For Jews, our time in Flossenbürg was up.

CHAPTER NINE: DEATH MARCH

I n the Flossenbürg station, we found a long train with two locomotives waiting for us. About sixty or seventy people were ordered into each car. It was a large transport, possibly with as many as two thousand people. Nonetheless, the cars weren't as crowded as some of our other trips, and we were able to sit down. SS officers were riding with us, and they kept a close watch on all the passengers.

The train started moving out. After only about two kilometers, there was suddenly a *flieger* alarm. The train had just pulled into the nearby city of Floss when it stopped suddenly as airplanes approached overhead. The Germans ordered us to run to the hedges beside the tracks. There were small farms bordering the tracks, and some of us managed to go beyond the hedges into the yards or houses. I saw a chicken sitting on some eggs. I chased off the chicken and grabbed two eggs. Others managed to find a potato or a piece of bread.

After the planes passed, the Germans yelled for everyone to get back onto the trains. Once we were inside the wagons, we all showed off our stolen treasures and hungrily consumed them in a single bite. Unfortunately, my eggs turned out to be worthless as there were little chicks inside. Soon we began moving again. We traveled for about fifty kilometers until the city of Schwartzenfeld. As we pulled into the station, two planes suddenly came in. Again we jumped off the train, but this time we were ordered to hide underneath the rail cars.

The planes circled like bees around us, shooting at everything in sight. The attack lasted for ten or fifteen minutes. A few Jewish prisoners were hit, and I think one SS officer too. When everything was quiet again, we were chased back onto the wagons. Finally, after a half hour, we were all assembled and ready to move again.

We rode on that train for two or three days. Maybe four. I don't remember if we received any food.

One morning, we arrived in Wiedenfeldstraße, a city about 100 kilometers from Schwartzenfeld. Suddenly, there was another *flieger* alarm. Five or six planes were coming in, but there was no time to move us all out. The SS jumped off the train but kept their guns pointed at us as they kneeled a short distance from the tracks. They warned that anyone who moved would be shot. We were simply to lay low on the floor of the cars.

As the planes approached, they aimed primarily at the locomotives, riddling them with bullets until they were completely destroyed. Since we were so exposed, a number of people were also hit during this attack. Bullets flew everywhere each time the planes passed over us. We may have lost forty or fifty people, though it was hard to tell because the train was so long.

This attack was particularly traumatizing for me since my friends were among those who were hit. I saw a big bullet, about five inches long, come flying towards us. It pierced the heart of Moishele from Klausenberg, who couldn't get low enough in the car. Then it went through Baruch Feig's jaw, before finally exiting through the side of the wall.

The bullet killed Moishele immediately. Afterwards, it took off Baruch's jaw but did not kill him. His jaw hung on a piece of skin, leaving his tongue exposed. It was a terrible sight.

When the attack was over, all the dead and wounded were taken out. Baruch Feig was placed with the others on the platform in front of the train.

In the meantime, several SS grabbed two people who had jumped off the train. There was a large field on the other side of the tracks with a small structure for storing potatoes. These men had escaped inside to grab a handful of potatoes, but unfortunately, they had caught the attention of a sharp-eyed SS officer.

The two men were pulled onto the platform and ordered to stand next to the bodies of the dead and wounded. One of the Nazis began screaming that we had already been warned that all those who plundered and stole during a *flieger* attack would be killed. He then proceeded to shoot the two people in front of the entire transport, making sure though not to kill them right away. They let them writhe on the ground in front of all of us before killing them with some additional bullets.

During all this time, Baruch Feig was lying on the ground in terrible pain. There was blood gushing from him and I could not bear to look in his direction. He was still conscious and pointed with his finger to his forehead, motioning for someone to have mercy and shoot him.

Leiby Hecht, who was from the same town as Baruch, somehow managed to make his way onto the platform to be with him. Baruch reached into his pocket and put two cigarettes into Leiby's hand. Each cigarette was worth a lot of money and could be bartered for precious items of survival. This was his parting gift to Leiby, who would hopefully be able to use the cigarettes to survive. He then pointed to his forehead again, begging Leiby to ask someone to shoot him.

Finally, an older German soldier took pity on Baruch. He leisurely took aim and shot the young boy in the head two or three times, bringing an end to his suffering.

My friends and I were devastated to lose two of our group in such a violent manner. However, we could not even allow ourselves to mourn or cry. Processing our pain was a luxury we did not have as we tried to remain focused on our own survival.

At first, we remained on the train as the Germans tried to figure out what to do next. At some point, every three men received one loaf of bread and some salty cheese. We were warned to save some of the bread since it would have to last for a long time. Afterwards, we were ordered to get off the train and assemble in the large open field near the train station. One of the Germans explained that all the railroad paths were closed off because of the repeated attacks. "We wanted to be nice and take you by train," he said, "but the Americans want you to go by foot."

The Germans said that anyone who could not walk should step to the side of the road to be transported by truck. By then we knew how the Germans like to "take care" of the sick and weak among us, so no one stepped aside. In the end, the German officer himself began picking out the weak people who could clearly not survive a long march. Among those were many people I knew, including my friend, Yossi Yakobovitch, his father, and another man, Yida Hersh Miller, all from the Visheves. There were others too whom I no longer recall. Tragically, Yossi Yakobovitch is the only one from this group who managed to survive.

As it turned dark outside, the SS divided the rest of us into groups of 200. We remained standing in rows of five, and each group of 200 was surrounded by SS officers to begin marching together. We were told that there would be no food until we arrived at our next destination.

Night fell soon after we started marching, but we continued going, for eight or nine hours. We were marching through the Bavarian region of Germany, not far from the Czech border. Luckily, I managed to stay together with Leiby Hecht, the two Hecht brothers, and another Polish boy. The five of us kept together throughout the march and looked out for each other like brothers.

At about four in the morning, we finally stopped in a small forest. We were told to lie down to rest. Fortunately, we hadn't lost anyone from our group of 200.

There was a little pond nearby but we were warned not to go near it to drink. Of course, we received no food either. Later in the morning, after we had slept, we were finally taken in groups of ten to the water to wash our faces and take a few sips. It was mid-April and the water was ice cold.

Soon we were on the road again. We walked for several hours before stopping. This time, everyone received eight potatoes and a spoonful of sauerkraut.

As the food was distributed, there was a lot of pushing and shoving. Everyone was starving and desperate for a bite to eat. The SS became enraged and started yelling at everyone. Tragically, one person was hit during this time. It was the first death of our group's march. (Two or three years ago, I was reminiscing about our war experiences with Mr. Mermelstein in Woodlake Village in Woodridge, New York. He reminded me that this man was shot because he stood in line twice to get a double portion of potatoes.)

We spent that night in a forest outside a small village. It was very cold at night but we had nothing to warm ourselves with. We were all shivering and trying to ignore the cold so that we could sleep.

The next morning, we received no food. Some people started tearing at the grass for lack of anything to eat. At around noon, we finally received potatoes again, though there was no sauerkraut. No one wanted to risk being shot at, so the food distribution was more orderly this time.

Sometime in the afternoon, an SS soldier told us that we would have to continue walking. There was no more food here, but the Germans hoped there would be bread in the next village.

During our walk, the skies suddenly opened and heavy rain began to fall. The SS went to the side of the road for shelter but we had to remain unprotected in the middle of the road. It dawned on me that we weren't much different from the horses in our village, which were also left in the rain while the wagon drivers looked for shelter during a downpour.

When the rain let up, we continued walking. The SS kept ordering us to walk faster and faster. We were moving so quickly that we soon passed other groups that had been walking all day. Every few minutes, we heard shots ring out. Soon afterwards, we began finding dead people on the side of the road about every ten or twenty yards. It was clear that the SS were killing whoever could no longer keep up.

We continued walking after dark, hearing intermittent shooting as we went. The rain also resumed and we were all cold and wet. It was a difficult night that some of us thought we would not survive. At some point we encountered a group of men who were sitting on the ground as graves were dug beside them.

The SS finally decided to stop on a road near Pösing, a town situated 105 kilometers (65 miles) from the Wiedenfeldstraße train station. There were some farmhouses in the area, and we had come upon two large barns that stood on either side of the road. The Germans ordered us to line up for *appel.* They counted us and determined that there were 170 people in our group. Thirty had been shot on the way because they had had no strength to continue.

The SS divided us into two groups, sending one to the barn on one side of the road and the second to the barn on the other side. I followed the Germans with the rest of my group inside one of the barns. We were told to lie down and rest and warned that the Germans would remain on guard outside. Presumably, they planned to take turns resting inside the farmhouse next door.

There were large stacks of straw inside the barn. As soon as the Germans left, we all took off our soaking wet clothes and spread them across the floor to dry. Then, we crawled into the piles of straw for warmth. Within minutes, there were piles of torn, wet clothing on the floor and shivering, skeletal men resting inside the straw.

We remained sleeping in that barn until the following morning, April 23, 1945. After daybreak, an SS officer came in and told us to get dressed. He said we would receive warm soup and then continue marching.

A short time later, another officer came in. He told us to line up, as we would first be counted and then served. We lined up at one end of the barn, but the Germans were not happy with the count. They believed one or two men were missing. They went towards the stacks of straw and stuck their bayonets inside, checking to see if they would hit anyone. When they were finally convinced that no one was hiding, they turned around and opened the large barn doors. As we were about to march out, we were met by a most shocking and welcoming sight: a line of American tanks. Our liberators had finally arrived!

The first moments after the Americans came into view were overwhelmingly chaotic. The SS seemed to disappear almost instantly. There was a white star on the soldiers' tanks, and for a moment we wondered whether our liberators were Russian. We knew all along that we were close to the American front, but the star confused us. People were running back and forth not knowing what to do.

Amid the chaos, the new reality finally sunk in. I turned to the two Hecht brothers who were standing beside me. "I think we're free," I said.

CHAPTER TEN:
A WAYWARD BULLET

There was a moment of joy and elation as I realized that our nightmare had finally ended. However, before I could celebrate, I saw a young soldier in the third tank raising his pistol and aiming it straight at me. He may have been confused by the warm pair of French army khaki pants I had "organized" shortly before leaving Flossenbürg. Or perhaps he spotted an SS soldier running behind me. (There was a dog house and chicken pen behind us where an SS soldier was discovered and shot only minutes afterwards.) I will never know what prompted his action, but he fired a shot in my direction. The bullet hit me just above my left knee and I fell to the ground.

The two Hecht brothers who were with me helped me up, and I limped together with them towards the road. At first, the soldiers motioned for us to stay back as they looked out for German soldiers. Before long, though, we all began swarming towards the tanks. The soldiers had wooden crates filled with army rations that were stacked one on top of the other on the tanks. The soldiers began ripping open the crates and throwing cheese, chocolate, sardines, beans, and other foods toward us. We grabbed the food and almost broke our teeth in our hurry to eat it all. Some people also filled their pockets and shirts with food. We kept motioning to the soldiers for more food. At last, they held up their empty hands. Some of the soldiers cried openly in compassion as they showed us that they had nothing left to give.

By now, the Hecht brothers and I had reunited with Leiby and the Polish boy. The five of us had stuck together throughout the march and now we began searching together for more food. As I limped along, one of the Hecht boys told Leiby, "Mendel was shot." I had a red spot right above my left knee, but all I desired was food and I could think of nothing else.

As we explored the area, we soon came upon an inn of some sort. There, the Polish boy found a bucket of sugar. Leiby Hecht came across a bottle of wine. We were still desperately hungry. With nothing to open the bottle of wine, we struck the neck of the bottle onto a small stone, breaking off the top. We poured the wine into the bucket of sugar and began taking handfuls of this mixture. Finding nothing else, we went back outside and started heading down the road. We were walking away from the front, in the direction from which we had come the previous day.

We felt a little drowsy from the wine and sugar but we kept going. By now, as my adrenaline wore off, I began feeling intense pain. I broke off a branch from one of the trees and used it as a cane so that I could keep walking. At about two in the afternoon, we found a large field that was filled with American soldiers. I saw a Red Cross sign there and went over to a soldier for help.

The soldier took out a pair of surgical scissors, and with two quick snips, the left leg of my pants fell to the ground. "What are you doing?" I cried. "You ruined my pants! I have no other one to wear!"

He laughed at my hysterical reaction and proceeded to examine the wound. He bandaged my knee and said something in English that I didn't understand. He motioned for me to remain there. Leiby Hecht wanted to look for more food. "Mendel, we'll come back for you," he promised me.

As I remained there with the soldier, I realized that he was waiting for an ambulance. Since none were appearing, he motioned for me to come to a nearby Jeep, where several soldiers were waiting for him. The hood of the Jeep was down and he picked me up and put me on top of it. He asked the other soldiers to hold on to me and began driving.

We drove a short distance, perhaps about five kilometers, until we arrived at a rectory. A field hospital had been set up inside, with army cots spread across the floor. There were about fifteen wounded lying there in all.

I was only fifteen-and-a-half at the time, newly liberated but separated from all my friends and fellow Jews. My leg was throbbing terribly as I lay there on an army cot on the floor feeling terribly lonely.

As it started turning dark outside, two liberated French prisoners suddenly appeared. "Are there any German soldiers here?" they asked.

One man raised his hand. He was obviously in great pain. As I turned to look at him, I realized that he was the German commander who had been in charge of my group of two hundred men. The two men grabbed hold of him and went back out, taking him with them.

Two hours later, at around nine o'clock, the same Frenchmen appeared together with a few American soldiers. It was pitch dark outside but they had returned to check again if more German soldiers had arrived. "No," one man said. "Someone was here before but he was taken away earlier."

"Oh, we shot him already," the men replied.

I remained in that field hospital for two days. From there, I was taken by the Red Cross to Cham, a town about thirteen kilometers away, also in the Bavarian region. There, the army had set up a military hospital in a gymnasium, or high school.

I was taken into a large auditorium in the makeshift hospital. There was a desk in the center of the room for the American officer in charge of the hospital. The rest of the room was filled with rows and rows of cots that held wounded soldiers and newly-liberated concentration camp survivors.

The Americans had recruited Hungarian doctors and male nurses who were prisoners-of-war to serve in the hospital. Shortly after I arrived, some of them picked me up to bathe me. I didn't trust them, since we had suffered greatly from the Hungarian army prior to our deportation. I began screaming loudly in protest, until an American sergeant came running. "What happened? Why are you screaming?" he asked in Polish.

I could not speak English at the time, but I had picked up some Polish from fellow inmates. Seeing that the sergeant spoke Polish, I was able to communicate with him somewhat. I made it clear that I was afraid of the Hungarian nurses and worried that they would drown me. I didn't want any of them to touch me.

The sergeant asked several American soldiers to undress me and put me into a tub of warm water. As soon as I was immersed in water, I was overtaken by intense pain and began screaming like a madman. My feet were frozen and the hot water felt like a hundred razor blades cutting into my feet.

The Hungarian doctor who was on the floor came running to see what had happened. He took one look at my grey feet, which had frozen during the march in the ice-cold rain, and yelled, "Take him out of there!" He instructed the men to prepare a cold bath instead. He told them to seat me on the edge of the tub and only allow my legs to reach knee-deep in the water. I sat like that for about a half hour until the pain subsided. (Incidentally, my feet are sensitive to cold until today. On very cold days, I wear two pairs of socks to avoid feeling pain in my toes.)

Later I was given some injections. An American doctor, a captain, soon came over to hear what was going on and why I didn't want to be treated by the Hungarians. He was actually a Jew and was able to speak a broken Yiddish. He tried to reassure me, telling me that the Hungarians were all working under American supervision. Nonetheless, he saw how terrified I was that they would kill me. He promised to try to have the American doctors take care of me.

I was taken out of the auditorium and transferred to the upper floor, which was filled with American soldiers who were being treated by American doctors. There was only one other former concentration camp survivor there with me.

Three times each day we received an army-issue meal, which came in a sectioned container. The compartments contained marmalade, bread, and eggs. As soon as I received my portion, I made one sandwich of everything and gobbled it down almost in a single bite. Meanwhile, the soldiers sat around barely touching their food. I stretched out my hand and they happily gave me their leftovers.

Within a day or two, the other liberated prisoner and I began feeling very sick. We kept using the bathroom, which led to dehydration. The American doctors soon came in to talk to the soldiers, apparently telling them that they could no longer share their food with us. Clearly, we were eating too much too quickly and risked jeopardizing our health.

The next time food was served, we shoved ours down our throats and then looked on enviously at all the leftover food in the soldiers' laps. Some of them began crying as they looked at us helplessly, knowing that they could not share their food with us. Before long, the orderlies came to take away their half-eaten plates.

After about a week, the American soldiers were transferred to a different hospital. Once more, I joined the general hospital population, which consisted of Ukrainian, Polish, Italian, Hungarian, and other survivors. There were only about ten or twenty Jews among the patients, and we all stuck together.

During all this time, I suffered terribly from pain and inflammation as my knee refused to heal. At first, I could only lie in bed on one side. Later, I started crawling around and eventually I learned to use crutches too. Each day, the nurses would put me up on the ledge by the window so that I could see the world outside. At times I felt terribly an-

---

gry as I saw German people going about their daily routine. They appeared happy and healthy, unconcerned with my suffering. It seemed so unfair that they could resume their lives while I continued to suffer.

One day, we were all in a big room that was filled with many patients, when two soldiers walked in. They were not American soldiers, but wore round berets and the uniform of the British Army. They were talking quietly to each other, as they circled the room carefully.

As they approached us, we suddenly realized that they had an insignia on their shoulders which said "Palestine." A moment later we realized that they were actually conversing in Yiddish! Before they knew what hit them, the two men were flat on the floor as the Jewish patients threw themselves onto the men in excitement. We were overtaken with emotion at the sight of young, healthy Jews who were dressed smartly in uniforms. Other than the American Jewish soldiers—who seemed to belong to another world—we could not believe that there were still European, Yiddish-speaking Jews who were not broken completely in body and spirit.

Once the British soldiers were back on their feet, they explained that they were searching for their families. They asked for our names and the names of our towns to see if any of us might have crossed paths with their own families. Unfortunately, none of us had any helpful information to offer them. However, during that exchange we did learn that there was another large camp named Bergen-Belsen, which was not too far away and also had many survivors.

One day, I was surprised by a most welcome visitor: Leiby Hecht. We were overjoyed to see each other again, though he could not remain for long. He was planning to continue to Bergen-Belsen, hoping to find surviving relatives. I also learned that his cousins, the Hecht brothers, had managed to join a youth transport and were heading to London.

Some days, when I felt a little better, I tried hopping around outside the gymnasium, hoping to find a familiar face. It was terribly frustrating to know that everyone was moving on and searching for family members while I was left all alone, confined to the hospital because of my injury.

In the middle of August, my pain became unbearable. My leg swelled up and I was no longer able to straighten it. The Jewish doctor, whose name I learned was Meir, informed me that I would have to be operated on immediately and promised to do the surgery himself. I was terribly frightened and kept crying, "I'm going to die! I'm going to die!"

I was the baby among all those survivors in the hospital, and the Jewish men had taken me under their wing. One older Hungarian man kept patting me on the arm and reassuring me that everything would be okay.

After I was wheeled into the operating room, I saw the Jewish doctor there, ready to operate as he had promised. However, I also saw the Hungarian doctor following us inside to assist him. I curled up in a ball and refused to allow them to treat me until that doctor was sent out. Meir began patting me and speaking to me softly in English, trying to calm me down. Although I could not understand his words, I felt the comfort and reassurance they were meant to convey. Nonetheless, I refused to change my mind. Ultimately, Meir called the head of the hospital to assist him.

The doctors gave me local anesthesia and covered me so that I wouldn't be able to observe their work. However, there was a mirror from which I was able to see that the Hungarian doctor was still there. I started crying until they finally sent him out.

After the surgery, the Jewish doctor carried me up to my room. I was in tremendous pain and could not focus on anyone or anything. My Jewish friends surrounded me and tried to comfort me. I heard them tell me, "Mendel, your brother is here." I said, "Yes, yes," not really believing or processing their words.

I was staring at the wall when I spoke, but when I turned my head to look at them, I saw that there were indeed two new faces. They belonged to my brother Tuli, and a dear family friend, Moshe Ganz. Tuli told me that he was in Munich with my father and Baruch, who had both also survived. It seems that in Bergen-Belsen Leiby Hecht had told a Yid from Ruscova that there was a young boy from Oyber-Visheve in a hospital in Cham. That person had continued to the Feldafing DP camp, and from there the news had traveled to my family.

Though I had been waiting for this moment for so long, I could not respond to Tuli. I was in a fog, overtaken by pain and still under the effect of the medication. Before I knew it, it was time for Naftuli to go. He said he would return to Munich to tell my father that I was alive and promised to come back in two weeks to pick me up.

Shortly after Tuli returned to Munich, in August of 1945, my father learned that a transport was about to leave for Romania. At the time, travel was very difficult, and a three-hour trip could take two weeks. My father wanted to take advantage of the transport and asked Tuli to go home to the Visheves to see if any family members had found their way back or if there was anything left to salvage.

Naftuli did manage to find several items, though some of them were confiscated when he crossed the Romanian and Hungarian borders on his way back to the American Zone in Germany. Ultimately, he brought back my mother's brass candelabras, the beautiful shawl she wore for *lecht tzinden* each Friday night, and my parents' engagement picture.

Of course, I did not know about these new developments. I was still alone in the hospital in Cham, confined to my bed for ten days. Soon after I was able to get up, I learned that the Americans were organizing a transport to the Feldafing DP camp. I was anxious to join my family and impatient to keep waiting for Tuli. I knew how difficult transportation was at the time. Who knew how long it would take him to make his way to Cham, which was 180 kilometers (about 112 miles) from Munich and required a two-hour trip during normal travel times.

The Feldafing DP Camp was located only thirty-four kilometers (twenty-one miles) farther than Munich. I made up my mind to travel there immediately, since I knew it would be much easier to reach my family from Feldafing than from Cham. The doctors did not want to let me go since I was still weak and my injury had not yet healed. Nonetheless, I could not resist the intense pull to join my surviving family members. Against their recommendation, I left the hospital and hopped on crutches for two or three kilometers until I reached the departure area. With the help of other Jews, I painfully climbed onto the back of an army truck that usually transported troops. When the truck finally began moving, I felt crushing pain each time it bumped over pebbles and potholes, but I was glad to finally be making my way towards Feldafing.

Towards the end of the trip, we passed the city of Munich. As I sat in the truck, I suddenly spotted my father and Baruch walking together. I screamed, "Tatte! Tatte!" but they did not see me. They were certainly not expecting to look for me on the back of an army truck in Munich!

I arrived in the DP camp in terrible pain. Nonetheless, I was excited to be surrounded by Jews in a place that almost felt like a real Jewish community. In fact, though the war had just ended, a *shul* had already been established there.

As soon as our transport arrived in the camp, we were besieged by desperate survivors eager to hear word of their loved ones. Every new arrival was cross-examined, as people wanted to hear where he had come from and whom he had seen.

In fact, I believe I was a good *shaliach* for one such desperate survivor. As I came off the truck, a middle-aged man asked, "*Efsher husti gezein tzvei Ungarische yingelech, einer azoi hoiech and einer zoi hoiech?*" He motioned with his hand approximately two inches apart, to show the height of his children, two Hungarian boys.

As he described them, I suddenly recalled seeing these Hungarian boys and hearing that they had joined a youth transport to London. As soon as I shared this information, the man ran off to make inquiries at the Red Cross.

Year later, I learned that this man was the grandfather of Dr. Chana Gelbfish, a respected pediatrician in Flatbush. In 1989 or 1990, I attended a dinner that was hosted by the Gelbfishes. During the event, I recognized an older man, who I learned was the uncle of the hostess. After making further inquiries, I learned that he lived in London, and indeed, he was one of the two young boys who was reunited with his father, after the man met me in Feldafing and followed his sons to London.

The Feldafing DP camp had served as a Hitler-*yugent* retreat and consisted of seven large two-story buildings, at least a dozen temporary buildings, and some large villas. One of the large buildings in the camp served as a hospital, and all who required medical treatment were cramped together in its large, main room. Shortly after my arrival, I was in so much pain that I realized I had no choice but to check myself into the hospital before I could make my way to Munich.

Fortunately, news of my arrival traveled quickly by word of mouth. Before long, my father heard that a young Tessler boy had arrived in Feldafing. Though he lived in Munich, preferring to remain outside the DP camp system, he was in regular contact with people traveling to and from the camp. As soon as he heard the news, he came immediately to see me. Strangely, I remember nothing of my reunion with my father and Baruch. I was consumed with pain and probably unable to process my overwhelming emotions.

I soon learned that my father had established a restaurant in Munich together with a partner, a Polish Jew by the name of Mendel Steinberg. This was after he had first worked on his own, catering weddings for survivors. He remained at the restaurant until our departure, and even hosted a two-day conference of all the *rabbanim* from the surrounding DP camps during that time.

Eventually, I heard a little more about my father's and brothers' war experiences. They suffered terribly while working in the Warsaw ghetto, and later endured a difficult trip to Dachau. My father was assigned to nearby Vald-Lager, where he landed in the camp hospital due to an infection in his leg. There, he was treated by a Jewish Hungarian prison-doctor, who called him "Tessler Batchie" and tried to help him as much as possible.

One day, the German decided to clean out the hospital and kill all the sick and wounded. Somehow, my father was left on his bed. An SS officer came in to walk through the hospital with the Jewish Hungarian doctor to make sure that all the beds had been emptied.

My father's mother, our *Babbe Fradel*, had loved my father very much. He was a big *masmid* in his teens and learned up to eighteen hours each day. Seeing how diligently he learned, his mother often prepared special foods for him and always tried to help him in any way she could.

As my father lay in his bed, weak and semi-conscious, he dreamt that he was trying to cross a river but somehow was unable to get across. Suddenly, his mother appeared in his dream, grabbed his hand, and crossed the river with him.

While my father was seeing himself at the river, the doctor had come into the room with the SS officer following close behind him. The doctor suddenly noticed Tessler Batchie in his bed and quickly pulled up the covers before the officer noticed. With his thin frame hidden beneath the cover, the German walked right past the bed, not realizing that someone was still there. The doctor, who would also survive and settle in Brooklyn, was terrified that the German would realize what happened. Afterwards, he could hardly believe that his dear friend Tessler Batchie had miraculously survived the hospital liquidation.

Though I heard the above story several times from my father, he actually spoke very little about his war experiences in general and didn't drill me for details either. He knew we had all suffered and didn't want to rock the boat by bringing up difficult memories.

Among the survivors, my father, who was in his forties, was considered an "older man." Young survivors from the Visheves, whose fathers had been friends of my father, would come to him for advice and support. They discussed *shidduch* prospects with him and asked for practical guidance as they tried to resume normal lives. They trusted him completely, and if they found gold, for example, they gave it to him for safekeeping.

I remember one young man who came to discuss a *shidduch* that had been suggested. A widow and her young daughter had survived, and someone had suggested this beautiful girl for him. However, the family was originally from Budapest, where life was very different from the Visheves. "How can this work?" he asked my father.

"Don't worry, about it," my father replied. "Everyone is really the same."

Indeed, the young man married the girl from Budapest, and later, he suggested her mother for my father. "I don't know," my father told him. "She's from Budapest…"

"That's what I said!" the man replied. "You told me that it's all the same. It doesn't matter."

"For young people it's different," my father replied. "For older people, it's not so simple."

Indeed, this young man, who eventually became a successful Manhattan jeweler, was but one of many people for whom my father lent a listening ear and offered words of support. Though he had lost his beloved wife and six of his children, and had also suffered terribly, my father seemed to have made peace with the tragic events. He was a man of deep faith, who believed that it wasn't his job to question, only to pick up the pieces and keep moving forward. There was an air of acceptance about him, as he devoted his energies to the future, working to establish himself financially so that we would be able to emigrate with his surviving sons at the earliest opportunity.

CHAPTER ELEVEN: HEALING TIMES

Several weeks after my arrival in Feldafing, there was much excitement in the camp as General Eisenhower was expected to visit. Hungarian prisoners-of-war were set to work to clean up the camp, and all the hospital patients received brand new red pajamas.

General Eisenhower's visit fell on Yom Kippur. He inspected parts of the camp and then everyone gathered outside to hear him speak. He addressed the crowd in English, and although we didn't understand a word, we all listened in awe to the great American general. I was there too, standing with my crutches among the crowd.

After the General spoke, the Klausenberger Rebbe stood up to address him, on behalf of the crowd. As I mentioned previously, he had been in the same *kommando* as my father and brothers and had also suffered greatly during the war. His young wife and ten of his children were murdered by the Nazis, and his eldest son, the eleventh child, passed away shortly after the liberation. Despite his own trauma and pain, the Rebbe became a powerful leader and a source of much *chizuk* to other survivors in Feldafing.

When the Klausenberger Rebbe stood up, a hush fell over the crowd. He had been *davening* in the *shul* with everyone and had come out before Mussaf to meet General Eisenhower. An American chaplain, the son of the Veitzerne *dayan* in Hungary, acted as the interpreter and translated the Rebbe's passionate words to the General. During his speech, the Rebbe asked General Eisenhower for three things: for more food, as there was a food shortage in the camp, for more hospital space, as dozens of army cots were crowded into one room, and for the General to intervene with President Truman to allow the Jews to immigrate to Palestine.

General Eisenhower expressed great interest in the plight of the Jews in the camp and promised to help. Everyone was impressed by his refinement and compassion, and we hoped that he would indeed be able to help us.

Only four days later, on Erev Sukkos, it became clear that General Eisenhower's concern was sincere and that he was indeed a man of his word. An entire battalion of Red Cross ambulances arrived in the camp and collected all the sick and wounded from the hospital. We soon learned that they had already transferred some 800 wounded SS officers from the nearby Hotel Kaiserin Elisabeth to a large prisoners-of-war camp outside of Feldafing. Now, they were taking all the patients from the overcrowded Feldafing hospital to the vacated hotel.

Hotel Kaiserin Elisabeth was a beautiful compound, which had been a favorite retreat of Empress Elisabeth of Austria. The hotel overlooked Lake Starnberg and was only two or three kilometers from the DP camp. The hotel had been converted into a hospital for wounded SS officers, who had enjoyed comfortable quarters there, with one or two beds per room. We were immensely grateful to General Eisenhower for turning it over for our use. We could now receive better care in a more spacious complex. The hotel had a large auditorium that became the exercise and therapy room, and its close proximity to the Feldafing DP camp was very convenient for the Jewish patients.

For the next three-and-a-half years, I moved between the Hotel Elisabeth hospital in Feldafing and my father's residence in Munich. I endured numerous surgeries as doctors tried to heal my injury, which ultimately also complicated our immigration efforts. Under the best of circumstances, it was very difficult to obtain all the necessary documents; however, for someone with an open wound or serious disease, doing so was virtually impossible.

The doctors in Feldafing were very concerned about my welfare because I was pale, weak, underweight, and in terrible pain. After numerous examinations they still could not figure out how to treat me, so they finally scheduled an exploratory surgery for October 10, 1945. The surgery lasted less than an hour but left me in terrible pain. The site of the incision kept bleeding and the dressings had to be changed frequently. I could not eat and started running a high fever.

After I felt somewhat better, the chief doctor met me and explained that I needed another surgery to remove the bullet completely. It was sitting in the marrow of the bone and preventing a full recovery.

I was operated on again on November 20. I was so weak afterwards that I could not lift my hand or take anything by mouth. Only on the third day could I finally drink some tea, though it would be another two weeks until I could eat bread and soup.

I was in a cast for one month and waited another month for my wound to close up. At last, it seemed that I had recovered completely. The doctor told me that I was ready to be released, and I made plans to catch the afternoon train to Munich. As I took leave from the doctor, he decided to examine my leg one more time. He was surprised to find that there was still pus gathering at the site of the surgical incision. To my dismay, he asked me to return my release documents. I had been anticipating returning to normal family life with my father and brothers and felt terribly depressed when I realized that my stay in the hospital was still not over.

I remained in the hospital for several more months until the doctors decided to perform another surgery on March 21, 1946. Again, the recovery was a slow, painful process that lasted several months.

I remember an incident that occurred, I believe, that spring, on Shavuous of 1946. An organization, probably the Joint, had arranged for a *sefer Torah* to be sent to Hotel Elisabeth for *yom tov*. All of us patients were very excited upon the arrival of the Torah, and our unabashed joy was much like a baby upon receiving a lollypop.

On Shavuous, we were eager to *daven* with the *sefer Torah*. When it came time for *krias haTorah*, we suddenly realized that there was no one among us who could *lein*. The majority of the patients were young men, and the few older ones who were there could also not *lein*.

We decided to take a Chumash and put it on the open *sefer Torah*, so that we could have the Torah open yet read the words out of the Chumash. After our initial excitement over this solution, we realized that we had yet another problem. No one knew which section of the Torah we were supposed to *lein*! At last, we decided to place the Chumash on top of the *sefer Torah*, open it up, and read whatever we found.

I will never forget that *yom tov* service, when a group of young, injured and sickly survivors were gathered together, overwhelmed with a desire to *daven* to Hashem to the best of their abilities.

Shortly after Shavuous, on June 13, I finally received my release forms again. However, my joy was short-lived, because after only a few days I was in terrible pain once more and had to return to my doctors in Feldafing. I was operated on immediately but received little relief. The doctors explained that my bone kept splintering. New bone shavings kept bringing on new pus and preventing the wound from healing properly. Despite my strong desire to move on with my life, I had to remain in the hospital to be under constant medical care.

In July or August of that summer, I had an experience that I will never forget. One Shabbos morning, the patients in the hospital learned that there would be a soccer match that afternoon between American soldiers and liberated Russian prisoners-of-war. The soccer match was scheduled to take place in Starnberg, a town only eight kilometers away. We could catch the train near the hospital and have an entertaining afternoon, relieving us of the drudgery of hospital life.

Though my father and brothers were visiting me as often as they could, I was quite isolated from my family and community. I was living amongst all types of people in the hospital and enduring a lot of pain, with little opportunity to focus on my Yiddishkeit. One day merged with the next, and while I considered myself a believing Jew, my religion was asleep for some time.

On that summer morning, I didn't even consider what day it was as I hobbled excitedly out of the hospital on my crutches together with the other mobile patients. We sang happily as we made our way to the station, thrilled at the opportunity to get out and mingle with the crowds.

When we arrived at the station, everyone was in high spirits, joking with each other. With exaggerated motions, we scratched our armpits and heads, pretending to be covered in lice. We laughed uproariously as the German passengers moved aside. Knowing their aversion to lice, some Jewish travelers found this an easy way to rattle the German passengers and secure a spot on the train.

Soon we could see the train approaching, and everyone prepared to board. Suddenly, a wind came out of nowhere and blew straight into my nostrils. The wind carried the smell of my mother's Shabbos food: her cholent, her *tzvibel mit ei*, her fish. Though no one was eating a Shabbos meal for miles around me, I was overtaken by the strong aroma of these foods. My arms dropped and my body grew heavy, as I leaned on my crutches for support. I stood there in a trance, like an outsider observing a scene in a movie. I watched the train pull into the station; I watched my friends from the hospital board the train; I watched the train depart.

When the train was gone, I suddenly came to, awakening from a dreamlike state. I realized in shock that it was Shabbos and I had almost boarded the train. How had that happened to **me**, someone who loved Shabbos and had experienced so many beautiful Shabbosim in my parents' home?

I turned around and started the two-kilometer trek back to the hospital. It had required immense effort to walk the distance on crutches in one direction, and I had expected a few hours off my feet before I'd have to do it again. I was hot and tired, and it seemed to be the longest, hardest, two kilometers I had ever walked. I just barely managed to make it all the way to the hospital. When I came inside, I fell upon my bed, unable to move, and cried for a long time.

That was a defining incident in my life. Thinking back to that period, I realize how easy it was for some young people, removed from family and friends, to simply follow the crowd without thinking. That overpowering smell of my mother's Shabbos food, a mysterious draft that came out of nowhere, shook me out of my reverie and put me back on track. I felt a newfound determination to live every day with conscious awareness of my faith and my future.

CHAPTER TWELVE: FINDING A HOME

I was impatient to resume normal life. So, in October 1946, after realizing that I was making no progress in the Feldafing hospital, I decided to visit the doctors at the Jewish hospital in Munich. I was examined in Munich by two orthopedists, a German doctor, Professor Brander, and a Jewish doctor, Dr. Pisochavitch. They explained that they would have to scrape the bone because there were many small metal pieces and bone splinters, and these prevented the wound from healing. Dr. Pisochavitch wrote a letter to the doctors in Feldafing, outlining a recommended course of treatment.

When I showed the letter to the chief doctor in Feldafing, he was very upset that I had gone to the doctors in Munich for a second opinion. "I'm sick for two years already!" I said in frustration. "I had to see if someone else can help me recover!"

When he calmed down, he explained that no surgery was necessary since the splinters would come out on their own. Nonetheless, he began taking x-rays more frequently to monitor the situation. After there was still no improvement, I returned to the doctor in Munich, who operated on January 20, 1947. Once more, I endured a difficult, painful recovery, but pus continued forming at the site of my injury.

During this time, my father continued working tirelessly to get us out of Germany. However, there was a quota of refugees per country, and there were only a few coveted slots for those from Romania,

Poland, and Hungary. Ironically, two-thirds of the immigration quotas had been allotted to Germany, from where there were very few Jews left seeking to emigrate.

Somehow, my oldest brother Naftuli learned that there was a Tessler family who had once lived in Breslau, Germany. Sadly, they had not survived, but their names were registered on official government documents. Naftuli succeeded in securing a refugee visa by claiming a spot as a member of this German Tessler family.

In the meantime, as it became clear that the immigration process would take longer for the rest of us, my father enrolled Baruch in *yeshiva*. He first attended one in the Zeilsheim DP camp, near Frankfurt, and later, the Klausenberger Rebbe's *yeshiva* in the Feldafing DP camp.

After some time, my father realized that the doctors' treatments were bringing no results. He recognized the urgency of finding a good doctor to treat me. After all, even if his efforts to accelerate the immigration process would bear fruit, I would be unable to pass the necessary medical examination as long as I still had an open wound.

After doing some research, we learned that there was a famous German orthopedist, a former general of the SS, by the name of Professor Max Lange. He was considered an expert in his field, and injured soldiers and civilians throughout the American Zone waited many weeks to see him.

My father and I felt that perhaps he was our best hope for a full recovery. We were desperate to see him immediately but could only get an appointment in three months' time. We arranged for Naftuli, who had recently arrived in the United States, to send a care package to the doctor's office to grease the wheels. There was a food shortage in Germany at the time, and only basic foods were available. Naftuli sent the professor a package containing several bars of chocolate, a few cartons of cigarettes, and a couple of pounds of Eight O'clock coffee. As soon as the package was delivered, in April of 1947, we called to schedule an appointment.

Thanks to our care package, the orthopedist saw me right away. He examined me and took x-rays and then recommended that I spend the entire summer sunbathing in the mountains. He instructed me to return in the fall and promised to operate then.

I followed his instructions though I saw no improvement at all. I returned after Sukkos, but somehow the surgery date kept getting postponed. First I developed rashes at the site of the injury, and when they finally cleared up, the doctor was about to leave for his holiday break.

Finally, on January 22, 1948, Professor Lange operated on me. Again, my leg was put in a cast and I was weak and feverish afterwards. Several days after the surgery, Lange's assistant changed the dressings at the site of the surgery. The next morning, I had terrible pains in my upper thigh. The pain became unbearable in the ensuing days, until Professor Lange took me back to the operating room. He opened the wound once more and discovered that the drainage tube he had inserted had become stuck. He cleaned the area and corrected the position of the tube. The procedure brought tremendous relief, bringing the pain down to bearable levels. After that incident, he didn't allow anyone to touch my bandages unless he was present.

During the entire time that I was treated by Dr. Lange, I was in a military hospital in Bad Tölz, not far from Hitler's infamous resort, the Eagle's Nest. The hospital was filled with recovering SS officers and German soldiers and I was terrified that they would poison my food or try to hurt me. I knew that I was under the strict supervision of Dr. Lange, but I did not feel safe until I left that hospital.

I was assigned to the last bed in a room with eight or ten beds. Most of the time, I sat with my back against the wall so that I was facing the room and could keep an eye on the other patients. I tried not to sleep too much so that I could remain vigilant. It seemed to me that the nurses and patients realized how scared I was and took pleasure in increasing my fears. For example, the nurses would repeatedly ask patients whether they could take their blood to check their blood type. "You don't need to take a test," the soldiers would respond, raising their arms. "I have my blood type marked here."

Indeed, the SS all had their blood types tattooed onto their arms, so that doctors would have the information in case of an emergency. However, the way the nurses kept asking this question with crooked smiles and the soldiers kept raising their arms, it seemed to me that they were simply trying to distress me and show that they were members of the SS.

After the operation, I remained in a cast for six weeks. Afterwards, I learned how to change the dressings on my wound on my own and was finally able to walk without crutches again.

Soon after I settled into a normal routine, I decided to sign up with the Haganah, which was recruiting young men to help with the fighting in Palestine. History was happening in the Holy Land, and I wanted to be there.

When my father found out about my plans, he went to the recruiting office and said, "When my son comes in, ask him to raise his pant legs."

"What?!" the men asked, confused.

"Just ask him to lift his pant legs," my father repeated.

Sure enough, as soon as the recruiters saw the dressings and realized that I had an open wound, they refused to accept me. I was deeply disappointed. "Why did you do this to me?" I asked my father.

"I already lost six children," he replied. "I'm not losing any more."

During all this time, my father continued running his restaurant and working on our immigration papers. He had several older brothers who had been living in America since the turn of the century, and they asked congressmen and senators to intervene on our behalf. We even received a certificate from our uncle, who agreed to act as our guarantor, but all these efforts were still in vain.

At last, on June 25, 1948, President Truman passed the Displaced Persons Act of 1948, allowing 200,000 refugees to enter the United States over a two-year period. As a result, my father was finally able to obtain visas for himself, Baruch, and me. However, our entry was contingent on a signed bill of health from a doctor, something that would still pose a challenge, since the site of my injury had not yet closed.

Fortunately, my father found an old German doctor who was a heart specialist and was connected to the American authorities. My father secured an appointment for the three of us on a Friday afternoon. He took along a nice sum of money, since he knew that this visit would not come cheaply.

The doctor examined us, but since he was a heart specialist, he focused primarily on our hearts. He didn't give us a full examination and never saw my wound. Instead, he asked my father whether he smokes and advised him to stop smoking.

After the exam, the doctor gave each of us a typed and signed letter, confirming our good health. With this letter and the newly-passed Truman Act, the door to America was finally open to us. After so much heartache and both physical and emotional pain, it was a relief finally to leave Germany behind us. Our departure was initially scheduled for Shabbos, with boarding set for Shabbos morning. The *rabbanim* in Munich *paskened* that all survivors who were able to travel with this ship were permitted to board on Shabbos. In the end, we did not have to rely on this *p'sak*, since boarding was moved up to Friday afternoon.

We departed from Bremerhaven, Germany, on the USS General Haan, a military transport ship, and arrived in America after a twelve-day journey, on Wednesday, Shushan Purim, March 16, 1949. We arrived in the afternoon when the harbor was closed, and there was no one to process the ship's passengers. We waited until the following day to disembark, finally stepping foot on American soil on Thursday, March 17, 1949.

Before disembarking, each passenger received a thick stack of pa-pers, which included questionnaires, medical forms, and other official documents. As soon as we stepped onto American soil, we had to hand over all these papers to a government official. We had no other docu-mentation with us, and many refugees refused to part with their papers. In Europe, papers often symbolized life, and now we were expected to enter a new country without a single official paper in our hands?

Representatives who spoke the native languages of all those on the ship were waiting for us at the harbor. They greeted each person and tried to reassure us in Polish, Russian, and Yiddish that it was okay to hand over all our documents to the officials. "You're in America!" they said. "Don't worry. You will receive new documents from the govern-ment."

Uncle Peter (Pinchas), my father's brother who lived on Ross Street in Far Rockaway, was waiting for us at the harbor. On the way to his home, he took us down Wall Street and explained that this was the richest street in the world. I remember looking up at the tall buildings and the black skies and wondering, *This? This is the richest street in the world!?* I had thought the American streets were paved with gold, but all around me I saw only black.

We also passed the Idlewild Airport (which was renamed in 1963 in honor of President John F. Kennedy after his assassination). All I saw were piles of mud, but Uncle Peter proudly informed us that this would soon be the largest airport in the world.

Uncle Peter was one of the founders and the president of the Old White Shul in Far Rockaway. My uncle put us up in the Hotel Gan-Eden, a hotel near his home, but my father, an authentic *shtetl* Yid, did not find his place in that community, which was too Americanized for him. On Friday, he took us to nearby Williamsburg, which was filled with other *heimishe Yidden*, European survivors like him.

To my frustration, my injury continued to torment me. After Shabbos, I checked into Beth Moses, a small hospital on Hart Street, in the Bedford-Stuyvesant area. I remained there for several weeks, as the doctors tried to heal my injury. During my stay, I became somewhat of a celebrity, after the doctors learned that I had been treated by Dr. Lange, who was a world-famous orthopedist. Once or twice a group of five or six doctors came down just to examine me and see the work of Professor Lange. One Czech doctor, a survivor now living in Canada, also made the trip to New York to examine me.

Ultimately, the doctors decided to give me aureomycin, which my cousin, Dr. Willie Berkman, explained to me was a new, experimental drug that had only recently been developed in the United States and was still in the trial phase. It was believed to be an effective antibiotic that could fight strains of bacteria that did not respond to other antibiotics.

The drug was administered every few hours under the careful watch of the doctors and nurses. It was a very toxic pill, and soon my entire body felt like it was on fire. I felt burning and itching underneath my nails, my eyelids, and skin. After about eighteen hours I could no longer tolerate it. In the middle of the night, when the nurse came with the next dose, I refused to take it. "That's it. I can't take it anymore," I told her.

When the orthopedist arrived in the morning, the nurses told him about my reaction to the pill and that I was no longer taking it. He came to my room and said, "We did everything we can for you. I have no other treatments to try. You'll have to make sure to change the bandages on your own, and I advise you to take only sitting jobs so that you don't aggravate your injury by standing or walking too much."

I left the hospital, determined to manage despite my injury and start a new life in America. Though I kept the doctor's words in mind, I did not succeed in finding sitting jobs. In fact, my entire life, I've always held jobs that kept me moving and on my feet. Nonetheless, I *did* manage and was always a diligent, hard worker.

CHAPTER THIRTEEN: BUILDING A NEW LIFE

B uilding a new life in *der goldene medinah* was no simple matter. At first, my father found an apartment for us on Columbia Street on the East Side of Manhattan, where many new refugees lived. My first job, which I found with the help of the Joint, was in a factory on the eleventh floor. I worked the night shift there and my job involved creating plastic seals for pocketbooks. I molded two pieces together with a hot iron that I operated by pressing a pedal with my foot. Not only was I on my feet the entire time, but I could only take the elevator on my way up to work. The elevator man, who was needed to operate the elevators in those days, left each day at six. I always made sure to arrive before he left, but when I finished my assigned work at two or three o'clock in the middle of the night, I slowly and painfully had to make my way back down eleven flights of stairs.

After a few months, we moved to 37 Lee Avenue in Williamsburg. Together with a partner, a man by the name of Preizler, my father opened a fruit store. Later, they expanded their product line to include fish too. The store was located in the storefront on the first floor, and we lived on the second floor, in an apartment above it.

At the time, the local police precinct was located right near our store. Every time the policemen walked by, we watched them anxiously from our window. We were scared to walk the streets and tried not to go out unnecessarily. Despite the reassurances of American acquaintances, we did not feel safe without any documents. Several months after our arrival, we finally received our green card, much to our relief. Our citizen papers arrived much later, five years after our arrival.

Once we felt somewhat secure and settled, my father began thinking about honoring the memory of our dear family members. A new Vizhnitz *shul* had just opened on 53rd Street in Boro Park, and my father decided to give a *sefer Torah* in honor of my sweet mother and innocent siblings who had died *al Kiddush Hashem.* I remember how we turned up that day, my father, Naftuli, Baruch and I. Everything was still new and raw, and to our dismay, we found construction debris inside the *shul.* We cleaned up the mess ourselves, shoving aside all the dirt, so that we could conduct a fitting celebration. The Vizhnitzer Rebbe from Monsey, *zul zein gezunt in shtark,* still lived in Williamsburg at the time, and he came in to Boro Park to officiate.

A short time afterwards, it was time for us, the surviving members of the family, to begin settling down. Within the next year or two, both Naftuli and Baruch got married. Naftuli and his wife ultimately settled in Chicago, where he became a successful businessman. Baruch and his wife remained in Williamsburg, where he became the Klausenberger Rebbe's devoted assistant, helping him establish the Klausenberg institutions there in the early years after the war. My father also became engaged shortly thereafter, marrying a Polish woman, Mrs. Dina Borg.[19]

A year or two after my father opened the store, he sold his share and bought a farm in Flemington, New Jersey. Many Jewish immigrants were purchasing farms in Flemington, Vineland, and other rural towns at the time. Farming was something they were familiar with from *der heim* and they hoped to find financial security through farm-

---

19   My father and his second wife were married for twenty-nine years and passed away just three days apart from each other. My father was almost ninety-four at the time and had merited to see his three surviving sons establish new generations of children, grandchildren, and great-grandchildren before his passing. He is buried in the Vizhnitz cemetery in Bnei Brak, Israel. His *matzeiva* also bears the names of my mother, Esther, and my six siblings who perished with her in Auschwitz. May Hashem avenge their blood.

ing in *der goldene medinah*. (Most of these ventures were ultimately not successful, and most Jews eventually sold their farms and moved back to Brooklyn.)

I also left Williamsburg and joined my father and his wife on the farm. We had seventy-two acres of land, with twenty-four cows and approximately two thousand chickens. I helped my father manage the farm and also took on a second job, managing J&J's famous milk farm, which was located nearby, in Frenchtown, New Jersey.

The work on the farm was very tough and demanding. Many times in the summer, the cows broke through the fence and went into the adjacent cornfield. Often, I'd hear crackling at two or four in the morning and had to jump out of bed to get them out before they did too much damage.

Another challenge during the summer was keeping the chickens cool. The chicken coop was too hot and I had to let them out to cool off. Afterwards, getting them back inside was a difficult job.

One time, we purchased three or four thousand little chicks that were only a few hours old. We paid between fifty and seventy-five cents for each one, an investment of a few thousand dollars. I was still inexperienced and forgot to turn on the heating lamps that keep baby chicks warm until they get their feathers. I left to attend a *chasunah* in New York, so I didn't check up on the chicks for some time. It was a cool night and the cold chicks climbed on top of each other to keep warm, stifling the ones on the ground. When I returned from the *chasunah,* I was horrified to see that I'd lost most of the chicks. Only one or two hundred survived from the several thousand that we had bought.

Farming was an all-consuming job that required twenty-four-hour dedication. On Shabbos, we had a non-Jewish worker who came to collect the eggs and milk the cows. The rest of the time I was busy with these and myriad other tasks.

At that time, there was a Bobover Yid, Usher Scharf, who owned the farm next to ours. His parents, R' Elya and Sura Scharf, visited him often, and we met with all of them from time to time. One day, Sura Scharf suggested a *shidduch* for me, Nusia Ehrlich, the daughter of her distant cousins. The Ehrlichs were also Bobover Chassidim and were originally from the town of Milewke, a suburb of Cracow in Poland. The Ehrlichs were an illustrious, *yichusdige* family. Rabbi Usher Selig Ehrlich was a tremendous *talmid chacham*, and a *yedid* and *chavrusa* of Rabbi Shlomo Halberstam of Bobov. Rebbetzin Sheindel Ehrlich was the daughter of Rabbi Aharon HaKohen Schantzer, the Milewke Rav, who was an old Bobover *chassid*. He was a genius of a man who was called to Cracow to lead the most difficult *din-Torahs*. In fact, the Kedushas Tzion of Bobov had been the Ehrlichs' *shadchan*.

The Ehrlichs had two children, Nusia (Necha Baila) and Chaim. The family had managed to escape from Poland and had spent the bitter war years traveling through Siberia. They suffered through freezing cold, starvation, disease, loss of home and family, and tremendous deprivation and degradation. They traveled from place to place with Rabbi Ehrlich acting as rabbi wherever they lived, his *sefer Torah* always at his side. The small family of four survived, and after the war they made their way to a DP camp in Traunstein, Germany, where Rabbi Ehrlich served as Rav and led *din-Torahs*, many pertaining to difficult and heartbreaking post-war issues like *agunos*. Eventually, the Ehrlich family immigrated to America in 1949, several months after us.

Despite the family's many struggles, Rabbi Ehrlich always made sure that Nusia continued her studies. Education was of paramount importance for this family. As a result, Nusia was fluent in Polish, Russian, and English, and proficient in literature and math.

At first I had some reservation about the *shidduch*. I didn't mind that the girl was Polish since I had learned to connect with people of all backgrounds during the war. However, I was a simple farmer at the time, and here someone was suggesting an educated, intelligent girl from a rabbinical family. I was also embarrassed about my lack of education, since my schooling had been cut short in my early teens.

After all, I had spent my teen years in camps and hospitals instead of in schools and *yeshivas*.

However, when I heard that Nusia had agreed to meet me, I decided that I had nothing to lose. *Vus ken shaten* one date?

When I met Nusia, I found her to be a beautiful, outgoing and intelligent young woman. She possessed a keen sense of humor but was very sensitive at the same time. She had a charismatic, engaging personality and was full of life. She had a special *chein* and was clearly beloved by all.

After a short courtship we became engaged, much to the joy of both our families. Though her father, Rabbi Usher Selig Ehrlich, was a *rav* and *talmid chacham*, he never *farhered* me or put me on the spot. On the contrary, he was an exceptionally warm person and always tried to make me feel comfortable. Her mother, Rebbetzin Sheindel Ehrlich, became like a mother to me.

Nusia and I were married on June 13, 1954, in the Hotel Diplomat in Manhattan. It was a beautiful wedding in a large and elegant hall that could accommodate the Ehrlichs' many friends and acquaintances.

After our wedding, I left the farm and settled in Brooklyn. We first rented a tiny, furnished apartment and later moved to 104 Hart Street in the Bedford-Stuyvesant neighborhood, a popular *frum* area at the time. Later we moved to a larger apartment in Crown Heights.

Since I'd been out of Brooklyn for some time, I had trouble finding work at first. My in-laws had promised to use their connections to help me with my job search but finding a good position turned out to be more challenging than they had expected. I took a series of menial jobs, doing whatever work I could find to support us.

A year after our *chasunah,* our daughter Esther Pesia was born, on March 11, 1955. It was especially meaningful for me to be able to name our baby after my *chashuve* mother. Both Naftuli and Baruch had only one girl each, and both girls were named after their wives' mothers, who had perished during the war. Since my mother-in-law had been fortunate to survive the war and was still alive at the time, Nusia was happy to name the baby after my mother. Indeed, my daughter was the only one to bear my mother's name until my brothers had granddaughters to bear her name too. The name Pesia was added for my father-in-law's, Rabbi Usher Selig's, mother. In those uncertain years after the war, people often felt the need to add names for other family members in case the future would bring more upheaval and there wouldn't be additional children.

Four years after Esther was born, we had our first son, Usher Selig, on February 28, 1959. He was named after my *chashuve* father-in-law, who had suddenly and tragically passed away a year-and-a-half earlier.

At around this time, I realized that I would have to learn a trade to support my growing family. I spent eight hundred dollars to take a printing course and learn offset printing.

After I finished the course, I took several different jobs until I finally found a good union job at a printing company in the Bronx, where I also learned color work. Though my salary increased, I still worked long, hard hours. The highway infrastructure was nothing like it is today, and my daily commute took about two hours on three different trains and two buses.

In those days, employees didn't dare ask to leave early on Friday. During the short winter Fridays, I could not always arrive home in time for Shabbos. For ten weeks each year, I stayed with my cousins, Esther (née Tessler) and Shimon Kopolowitz, who lived in the Bronx. Nusia and the two little children remained home alone on all those Shabbosim until I could join them on Motzei Shabbos. This was unbearably difficult for all of us, but we never complained. We were grateful that I had a good job and earned a decent wage.

Around this time, Esther was ready to start school. Nusia made some inquiries and then shared with me the advice that she had received regarding how to behave when she registered Esther in school. She had been told to get dressed in *shmattes*, make a sour face, and explain how her husband was making a living with difficulty. In this way, people explained, she would get away with paying almost no tuition.

When I heard her words, I became very emotional and started crying. "After I survived Auschwitz, and we are now *zoche* to send our child to *yeshiva*," I said, "I want you to get dressed in Shabbos clothes and take our W2 form to show exactly how much I earn each year. Show them that I'm earning $5,200 annually now and tell them that I can try to pay $20 per month for tuition."

Nusia did as I asked her. When she came into the office of Rabbi Levi's Bais Yaakov, known today as Bais Yaakov d'Rav Meir, she put down the W2 form and offered to pay $20 per month. The people in the office did not want to look at the form and immediately agreed to her offer. Later, we learned that most people paid $8 or $10 per month, and a few paid $12. Nonetheless, I never regretted not trying to bargain when it came to my children's tuition, and I believe that our attitude towards their schooling is what helped us have success with our children, *baruch Hashem*.

On January 6, 1965, my wife and I were blessed with a second son, Aron, who was named after my mother-in-law's illustrious father, the Milewke Rav, Rabbi Aharon HaKohen Schantzer. Rabbi Schantzer, from Tishmenitz-Stanislav, was a *chashuve*, brilliant individual, who was killed in the Bochnia Ghetto after the bunker he was hiding in with his family was discovered.

Now, with three children at home, the long commutes and Shabbos separations were becoming even more difficult and unbearable. Additionally, my oldest daughter was already ten years old, and I realized that as long as I remained an employee, I would not earn enough to marry off my children and support them as generously as I wished.

I finally decided to take the plunge and open my own company,

Mendy Press. I searched for a suitable location close to my home and borrowed money to purchase the expensive printing machines necessary to run my own company.

In November 1965, I was finally ready to open shop. Though I was still schlepping heavy skids and putting up with the loud, noisy machinery, at least now I was working for myself.

It had taken courage and perseverance to start my own company, and I *davened* to Hashem to reward my efforts with success. But, like all beginnings, starting my business was far from easy. Sometimes Nusia would call me at work and say, "Mendel, you didn't give me any money." I'd always say, "Oy, I forgot. I'll give you money before I leave for work tomorrow." In truth, I hadn't forgotten to give her money for food and household expenses. I simply didn't have any cash on me.

One day, as I was struggling to establish my business, Rav Meir Levi called me into his office. "Mr. Tessler, I don't want you to pay tuition for a while, until the business is on its feet," he said.

Most likely, Nusia told him that I had just started a business and was hardly making a living. However, since I did not want to take advantage of my daughter's school, we agreed that I would print all the school's yearbooks, stationery, and pamphlets at no charge, in exchange for having Esther attend Rav Levi's Bais Yaakov, as well as his summer camp, Camp Chedva. Printing all those yearbooks and paraphernalia was a huge undertaking that saved the school hundreds of dollars each year. Though it took hours of work and expensive supplies to fulfill my part of the deal, I was happy that my daughter was able to attend such an excellent school and one of the most popular camps at the time.

Three years later, when Esther was in the eighth grade, Rav Meir Levi was struck by a car one evening while walking to a board meeting. He never recovered and tragically passed away the following year. His son, Rabbi Michoel Levi, became the school's principal, and I continued the yearbook arrangement with him.

Rabbi Michoel Levi was only in his early twenties at the time of this tragedy. He was dealing with the shock of losing his father in such a violent, unexpected manner, while also trying to learn how to run a girls' school. During that difficult and challenging period, Rabbi Levi made countless visits to my printing shop. Perhaps the initial visits were related to the yearbooks, but eventually, he'd just drive to Manhattan after school was over and come up to talk. We developed a warm relationship over those printing machines, and until today, when I attend Siddur and Chumash plays or the graduations of my great-granddaughters, Rabbi Levi embraces me warmly and thanks me again for my support all those years ago.

Incidentally, I continued printing the yearbooks for a number of years, even after my daughter graduated. Thus, the school only gained from Rav Levi's thoughtfulness. He had wanted to help me when business was tough, but in the end, our arrangement turned out to be a good deal for the school.

As I began building my business, one of my earliest customers was Artscroll. I printed the book cover for their very first publication, a Megillas Esther that sold over a quarter million copies! Later, I printed the colored covers for about two dozen other books that followed.

One memorable incident occurred shortly after I opened my business. I received a call from Reb Shlomo Neiman, a Vizhnitzer *chassid* who lived in the then newly-formed Vizhnitz community in Monsey. His family was also originally from the Visheves, and we knew each other well. Shlomo had a bindery, so we often talked about the printing business and referred customers to each other.

That day, Shlomo called to ask me for a donation. He explained that the *bachurim* in the new Vizhnitz *yeshiva* in Monsey were studying in a small room that did not have adequate lighting. He wanted to install light fixtures so that the room would be properly illuminated. The cost, Reb Shlomo explained, would be $400 for the materials. Since one of the *bachurim* knew how to do the installation, there would be no additional costs. "Would you give us seventy-five dollars towards this project?" he asked.

I was still working to establish my own business at the time, and my first thought was to offer twenty-five dollars. However, as Reb Shlomo talked about the boys' learning and the inadequate lighting, I suddenly recalled the words of my grandfather, the staunch Vizhnitz *chassid* Reb Shmiel Chaim Rosenfeld: *"Bei aza sheine licht, vi ken men shlufen?"* I remembered his visit to my childhood home and how much he had enjoyed learning by the light of our newly installed light bulb.

"You know what? I'll give you fifty dollars," I said.

As soon as the words were out of my mouth, I reconsidered my donation once again. I envisioned my grandfather, looking down from the *Olam HaEmes*. How much pleasure he would take in knowing that I had provided the light necessary for young men to study Torah in the Vizhnitz *yeshiva* in Monsey!

"I changed my mind. I'll sponsor the whole thing for $400," I said, surprising even myself.

Of course, Reb Shlomo was grateful for my generosity and thanked me profusely. As soon as I hung up the phone, a non-Jewish customer walked in. "Mendy, I need you to price a job for me," he said.

I didn't particularly enjoy working with this customer because I usually had to wait a long time until he paid me for my work. Nonetheless, I listened to what he wanted me to do and calculated how much it would cost. To my surprise, the total came to the same amount that I had just pledged to Reb Shlomo! After I started working on the job, the customer added some other things to his order, bringing the total to about $250 more. The greatest surprise, though, came when the job was complete and the customer paid me immediately. I was certain that this was no coincidence and that my grandfather had approved and *shepped nachas* from my generous donation.

Over the next few years, I worked long, hard hours so that my company, Mendy Press, would develop a good reputation and attract a large customer base. *Baruch Hashem,* I managed to repay my loans and support my family. In the summer of 1971, we were finally able to move from our rented apartment in Crown Heights to our own home in Flatbush, where I still live today. Incidentally, Leiby Hecht also moved to Flatbush, and our paths crossed periodically.

As our children grew, their *chinuch* was the primary focus of our lives. Nusia lived her whole life for the children, and "*Aless far di kinder*" ("Everything for the children") was her oft-repeated cry. While we had the normal differences that exist in every marriage, we were of one mind when it came to our children's *chinuch*. We tried to provide them with a loving home, but we did not pamper them. We were strict but fair and understood that it was our job to educate our children. We weren't afraid to tell them what to do and what not to do, and we were not afraid to say "No." We taught them not to be wasteful and to appreciate everything they had. We wanted them to learn to be responsible, grateful, self-sufficient human beings.

When it came time to send the boys to *yeshiva,* I felt they needed to get away from "the *mamme's fartech,*" the mother's apron strings. I believed that in order for boys to learn properly and become *mentchen,* it was necessary for them to spend time away from home.

At first, my older son resisted the idea of going away to a dormitory. "Selig'l, I want this for you," I tried to explain to him. "In twenty years, we'll talk about it. Then you'll understand."

I looked into many different *yeshivas* and finally settled on Telz Yeshiva in Cleveland. The *yeshiva* had a summer camp too, so we decided to send Selig to camp as a trial, and then he would stay on if everything worked out. In the end, he stayed in Cleveland for four or five years and the experience shaped him into the exceptional person that he became.

Although many people sent packages for their children in *yeshiva,* we did not do so. We made sure that the boys received plenty of good food from the *yeshiva,* and when Selig sometimes complained that there was always chicken on the menu, I said, "Mommy and I would have been happy to have chicken every day in the camps and in Siberia."

Nonetheless, to make sure that Selig felt part of the family, we promised to keep him posted on all happenings at home. "When Esther starts dating," I told him before he left, "we'll tell you exactly how tall or short every young man is and whether his hair is red or brown."

The cost per minute of long distance calls was exorbitantly high at the time, yet I insisted that Selig call home often. I believed that it was worth spending a few dollars so that my son could hear family news and wish us "*Ah gutten Shabbos.*" In fact, those regular calls with Selig and our other children set a pattern for life because today I speak to all my children every day.

Though I usually did not close my printing shop for vacations and such, I made an exception when it came to Selig. I often flew to Cleveland to visit and spend time with him. When Nusia wondered how I managed to make the time, I explained, "When a child is away from home, I have to make an extra effort to give him *chizuk.*"

On one of my visits, Selig found a place where we could both sleep at night. After spending some time together in the evening, he asked, "Daddy, do you mind if I leave you here and you go to sleep on your own?"

"Where are you going?" I asked him.

"I have a *shiur* that I go to now," he said. "I will be out until 12:30."

His response was my reward, the payoff for all those years apart, and for pushing him to go away even when he didn't understand my decision. I was deeply touched to see how dedicated he was to his learning. Indeed, it didn't take twenty years for him to agree that it had been wise to send him away from home to learn.

When it was time to send Ari to yeshiva, I also sent him to Telz initially, since Selig had been so successful there. However, Ari had a tough *rebbe* and he had a hard time adjusting. He called me several times to tell me that he is not happy and the *rebbe* is too hard. He was a conscientious student who liked to do well and was frustrated that success seemed impossible.

I made some calls to Rav Gifter, *zt"l*, about transferring Ari to another shiur. One intense day of conversations cost me as much as $96 in long distance charges! Rav Gifter promised to address the issue, but said, "Just give me a few weeks so that things settle first."

Meanwhile, Ari, who had always been a determined child with an independent mind, decided that he'd had enough. He packed his things and borrowed money so that he'd have enough for the trip back home. He walked into the house with a list of the people to whom he owed money.

When Ari came home, I put my business aside and devoted myself to finding an appropriate *yeshiva* for him. There were some that Ari wanted to attend but I didn't feel were a good fit, and others that I wanted but Ari didn't like. We finally settled on Philadelphia, and *baruch Hashem*, Ari was extremely *matzliach* there. He also developed a strong connection with the Rosh Yeshiva, Rabbi Shmuel Kamenetsky, which he maintains until today.

Throughout this time, my injury kept flaring up periodically. Though the bullet had been removed in Germany, I had developed osteomyelitis, an infection of the bone. I visited many doctors and hospitals, hoping to find relief. In all, I endured ten operations from the time of liberation and countless treatment protocols, including the experimental one that had to be stopped. Nothing proved effective.

About twenty-five years ago, I finally met Dr. Sherry, a famous orthopedist. I endured the tenth surgery while under his care, and advances in medicine made it possible for him to vacuum the site of my surgery. While bone fragments and shrapnel were removed, some tiny pieces still remained.

A short time later, I met a Jewish immunologist, Dr. Hirschman.

He examined my injury and prescribed a new medication that he had developed, which was not yet on the market. That treatment was finally successful, ridding me at last of the bacteria that had festered at the site. Afterwards, the wound finally closed off, and for over two decades, I have no longer suffered pain or flare ups.

I never would have imagined that it would take four decades for my injury to be healed, but I managed to live an active life despite my injury and was grateful when relief finally came.

CHAPTER FOURTEEN:
MY BEAUTIFUL FLOWER GARDEN

Today, I am still incredulous when I consider my difficult journey that began at the young age of fourteen, and the suffering that followed even after I was liberated. There was a time in my life when I truly believed that the Jewish People had been wiped out and only a handful of individuals had survived. Sometimes, when I see young Jewish women with baby carriages, or young Jewish children playing in the street, I choke up as I recall the tragedies I have witnessed and marvel at the rebirth that has occurred in my lifetime.

In fact, whenever I say *Tachanun*, tears fill my eyes as I recite the paragraph of Shomer Yisrael. When I say *"Shomer Yisrael, sh'mor sh'eiris Yisrael, v'al yovad Yisrael"* these words are not empty words for me. I often feel goose bumps on my arms as I pray for Hashem to protect the Jewish People, to watch over those who have survived, and not allow the Jewish People to be lost forever. I have witnessed the devastation wrought by those who want to destroy us and I know how much we depend on the Guardian of Israel to protect us.

I often wonder from where I took the strength to rebuild and the knowledge to raise a family and give a proper education to my children. I believe that I was able to accomplish so much in my life because of the upbringing I received at home before the war and the devotion my father showed me afterwards, despite his own suffering.

My father lost his wife, who was only thirty-nine when she was murdered, and six little children, three boys and three girls between the ages of four and twelve. Nonetheless, he cared for me after I was injured without a word of complaint and without mentioning his own suffering during the war. He accepted all that had happened as having been decreed Min HaShamayim, with no questions. His inner strength and strong faith, despite all he went through, gave us surviving sons the courage to go on, and I will forever be grateful for that.

Though my parents and grandparents are long gone, my brothers and I were fortunate to be reunited with three old *seforim* that had belonged to our family in Romania, through a series of unusual events and extraordinary *hashgacha pratis*.

The first was a Sefer Tehillim that had an inscription from my grandfather, Reb Shmiel Chaim Rosenfeld. He had presented it as a wedding gift to a nephew in the 1930's. A cousin found it in Eretz Yisrael, and he gave it to my brother, who gave it to me.

The other two finds were even more meaningful and miraculous. Somehow, two *Mishnayos* that had belonged to my father in Romania made their way across oceans, all the way to our family.

About forty-five or fifty years after the war, my brother Naftuli was visiting Eretz Yisrael for *yom tov*. During his trip, he was approached by a man who handed him an old *Mishnayos Zeroim*, saying, "This belongs to you." Imagine Naftuli's surprise when he opened the *sefer* and found our father's name inside, with a list of all the nine children's names and birthdates in his handwriting! Apparently, someone found the *Mishnayos* in the Visheves after the war and took it with him to Eretz Yisrael. After years of use there, this man came across it in some warehouse, recognized our family name, and returned it to Naftuli.

Four or five years later, Baruch's son was in the Vizhnitz *shul* in Williamsburg, which, incidentally, stands on the spot where the police precinct once was, next to the shop that my father owned. Incredibly, he spotted an old *Mishnayos* in a pile of *sheimos*, and by chance, he picked it up and opened it. There, on the inside cover, he found the name of my father, his grandfather!

These findings have been incredibly meaningful to my brothers and me. They provide a physical link to the world that once was and are cherished by our entire family.

Over the last few decades, my family has grown and multiplied, *baruch Hashem*. We have merited much *brachah* and success with our children, perhaps due to the *tefillos* of our illustrious grandparents in the Olam HaEmes.

My oldest daughter, Esther, lives a few blocks away from me in Flatbush. Incredibly, she married her husband, Mutty (Mordechai) Alter, on Tu B'Av, exactly 50 years to the day that her namesake, my mother Esther, had married my father. Moreover, she has been blessed with six children, three boys and three girls. When her sixth child was born, I was overcome by emotion and could not stop crying to my daughter, "Esther and her six children are back! I have them back!" Today, they are all married, *baruch Hashem,* and are establishing beautiful families in New York and the surrounding areas.

Every year, I travel to Monsey to be with the Vizhnitzer Rebbe for Yom Kippur. I am both humbled and proud to be accompanied each year by some of Esther's sons and grandsons, continuing a family tradition of hundreds of years.

My son Selig lives with his wife, Betty, and their nine children in Eretz Yisrael. Selig has exceptionally *chashuve* children who are outstanding *bnei Torah*. One of Selig's sons is an officer in the IDF. It gives me much Nachas to know that while I was unable to join the Haganah and fight in Palestine, today one of my grandsons is protecting the Jewish people and Eretz Yisroel.

My son, Ari and his wife, Naomi, also live in my neighborhood in Flatbush. They have six wonderful children, and they and their families are all a source of much *nachas*. Ari is a successful businessman, and despite his busy schedule, he is immersed in *tzeddakah v'chesed.*

When my oldest grandson was Bar Mitzvah, I began a tradition that has continued until today. I make sure to buy a pair of *tefillin* each time a grandson or great-grandson turns thirteen. After my own *tefillin* were stripped away from me in the courtyard of Birkenau, I did not wear *tefillin* for several years. Even after the war, it was difficult to acquire *tefillin.* I am making up for that period each time I buy a pair of *tefillin* now. Today, when I count my *tefillin* and those of my sons, grandsons, and great-grandsons, I know that I am "wearing" at least twenty-five pairs of *tefillin* each day. That thought brings me immense comfort.

At every family *simchah,* my children and I ask the orchestra to play "*Am Yisrael Chai.*" I place a grandchild or great-grandchild on my shoulders and I dance in the middle of the circle with the members of my family surrounding me and dancing around me. This is a special moment at every family event, when I celebrate my beautiful family and Hashem's promise for Klal Yisrael's eternal survival.

At the time of this writing, two years have passed since the passing of my dear wife Nusia, in January 2015. I am grateful to Hashem for the many happy years we spent together and for giving us the opportunity to see our children grow up and establish their own beautiful families.

I began life in Marmorosh, a region that the Baal Shem Tov called "a beautiful flower garden." I will always cherish the memories of my childhood home and mourn the beauty that the *rotzchim* destroyed. I am grateful to Hakadosh Baruch Hu for allowing me the privilege to replant part of this beautiful flower garden. It is only through *emunah* in Hashem and devotion to His Torah that I have survived and have found the strength to rebuild.

”מִמִּצְרַיִם גְּאַלְתָּנוּ, ה׳ אֱלֹקֵינוּ, וּמִבֵּית עֲבָדִים פְּדִיתָנוּ,
בְּרָעָב זַנְתָּנוּ, וּבְשָׂבָע כִּלְכַּלְתָּנוּ, מֵחֶרֶב הִצַּלְתָּנוּ, וּמִדֶּבֶר
מִלַּטְתָּנוּ, וּמֵחֳלָאִים רָעִים וְרַבִּים וְנֶאֱמָנִים דִּלִּיתָנוּ. עַד
הֵנָּה עֲזָרוּנוּ רַחֲמֶיךָ, וְלֹא עֲזָבוּנוּ חֲסָדֶיךָ...“

(נִשְׁמַת)

"You redeemed us from Egypt, Hashem our G-d, and
liberated us from the house of bondage. In famine You
nourished us, and in plenty You sustained us. From the
sword You saved us; from plague You let us escape; and
from serious and lasting diseases You spared us. Until
now Your mercy has helped us, and Your kindness has
not forsaken us."

ACKNOWLEDGEMENTS

My heartfelt gratitude to my children and grandchildren
for their enthusiasm, their invaluable input, and the
endless hours they dedicated to bringing this project
to fruition. Reading the manuscript countless times,
suggesting, correcting, improving and refining, they
pooled all their literary, technical, computer and legal
skills in a concerted effort to help the book take shape.
Ever devoted and supportive, I know they are always
there for me.

I would like to thank Mrs. Shaindy Perl
who went above and beyond in helping me write
this book. I felt encouraged by her precise expertise,
competent guidance and commitment to accuracy.
With unfailing kindness, patience and insight, she
portrayed my life story as no one else could have.

Mendel Tessler

LETTER FROM MY CHILDREN

Dear Daddy, עמו״ש

Everything we are and everything we have is because of you and Mommy and the *Zechus Avos* you represent. Your life has always been a *Limud* for us all to emulate. A pillar of strength, you devoted your life selflessly and tenaciously to our care and guidance throughout the generations. We can never hope to fathom the self-sacrifice involved, nor to express our gratitude and appreciation adequately.

You taught us good values and *Midos* by constantly talking to us, patiently sharing with us, and mostly by setting a shining example. You taught us the meaning of family. You would regale us with stories of our *Babes* and *Zeidies*, our aunts and uncles, stories of *Der Alte Heim*. Not only did you tell us the tragic stories of how they died, but, more importantly, you told us the glorious stories of how they lived, recounting tales and anecdotes, painting scenes and personalities. These stories provided us with a solid grounding and stability so that we never felt alone or disconnected, because, surely, those *Neshomos* were watching over us and guiding us. We were taught that we represent them in this world and therefore we must never disappoint them or shame them. This has always been the bedrock of our existence.

Your zest for life is infectious and your hope for the future unending. You are the embodiment of עבדו את ה׳ בשמחה. It is an honor to watch you embrace each mitzvah wholeheartedly and with such relish. There is no one who portrays the *Midah* of שמח בחלקו better than you. Your love for the Torah and *Mitzvos* and for your fellow *Yid* is overwhelming. When you hear of a צרה, you truly share in the pain, and when you attend a שמחה, it is with your whole heart. Indeed, our

---

own *Smachot* are made all the richer and more meaningful as they are reflected in your eyes. All this goes into the foundation of our future generations.

Though you lived through גפרית ומלח שרפה כל ארצה, you persevered and thrived because בחרת בחיים למען תחיה אתה וזרעך. With an iron will to live and survive, and with fierce and unwavering courage, you were determined to continue the Golden Chain of *Am Yisroel*. You replanted the garden with salty tears, and, בלב שמח, you nurtured it for decades with hope and prayer. The seedlings had to be nourished, no matter the effort, no matter the cost. With steadfast love, *Emunah*, and *Yirat Shomayim*, you taught us to give *Tzedakah*, to sacrifice for another Jew, and to thank *Hashem* for everything He gives us. *B"H*, you are reaping now from that garden and have seen and will continue to see strong and beautiful *Peyros, b'ezras Hashem*.

אילן אילן במה אברכך ?...
שיהיו פירותך מתוקין, הרי פירותך מתוקין...
יהי רצון שכל נטיעות שנוטעין ממך יהיו כמותך

We wish you *Gut Gezunt, Koach, Arichus Yomim v'Shonim*, and *Grois Nachas - Nachas* that you should have from us, and *Nachas* that we should have from you and together with you, *Ad Meah v'Esrim Shana*. And Mommy, ע"ה, your עזר כנגדו for 60 years, will surely be a מליצת יושר for all of us as she watches over us from *Shomayim*.

With awe, reverence, and appreciation,
Your loving children,
Esther Pesia, Usher Selig, and **Aron**

FAMILY TREE

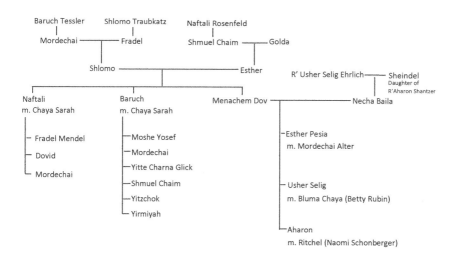

Baruch Tessler

Mordechai ———— Fradel
Shlomo Traubkatz

Naftali Rosenfeld

Shmuel Chaim ———— Golda

Shlomo ———————————————— Esther

R' Usher Selig Ehrlich ———— Sheindel
Daughter of
R'Aharon Shantzer

Naftali
m. Chaya Sarah

- Fradel Mendel
- Dovid
- Mordechai

Baruch
m. Chaya Sarah

- Moshe Yosef
- Mordechai
- Yitte Charna Glick
- Shmuel Chaim
- Yitzchok
- Yirmiyah

Menachem Dov ———————————— Necha Baila

- Esther Pesia
  m. Mordechai Alter
- Usher Selig
  m. Bluma Chaya (Betty Rubin)
- Aharon
  m. Ritchel (Naomi Schonberger)

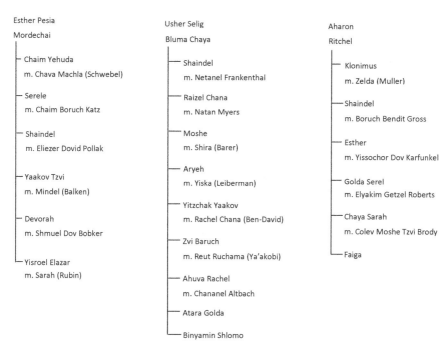

Esther Pesia

Mordechai

- Chaim Yehuda
  m. Chava Machla (Schwebel)
- Serele
  m. Chaim Boruch Katz
- Shaindel
  m. Eliezer Dovid Pollak
- Yaakov Tzvi
  m. Mindel (Balken)
- Devorah
  m. Shmuel Dov Bobker
- Yisroel Elazar
  m. Sarah (Rubin)

Usher Selig

Bluma Chaya

- Shaindel
  m. Netanel Frankenthal
- Raizel Chana
  m. Natan Myers
- Moshe
  m. Shira (Barer)
- Aryeh
  m. Yiska (Leiberman)
- Yitzchak Yaakov
  m. Rachel Chana (Ben-David)
- Zvi Baruch
  m. Reut Ruchama (Ya'akobi)
- Ahuva Rachel
  m. Chananel Altbach
- Atara Golda
- Binyamin Shlomo

Aharon

Ritchel

- Klonimus
  m. Zelda (Muller)
- Shaindel
  m. Boruch Bendit Gross
- Esther
  m. Yissochor Dov Karfunkel
- Golda Serel
  m. Elyakim Getzel Roberts
- Chaya Sarah
  m. Colev Moshe Tzvi Brody
- Faiga

Yahrzeits

נעכא בילא בת הרב ר' אשר זעליג - כ"א טבת תשע"ה 2015

שלמה בן מרדכי טעסלער - ה' כסלו תשנ"ב 1991

אסתר בת שמואל חיים רוזענפעלד - ג' סיון תש"ד 1944 - בירקנאו

גאלדא בת שלמה

צבי בן שלמה

פראדיל בת שלמה

יהודה מאיר בן שלמה

טובה גיטל בת שלמה

משה יצחק בן שלמה

ג' סיון תש"ד 1944 - בירקנאו

שמואל חיים בן נפתלי רוזענפעלד - ב' סיון תש"ד 1944 - בירקנאו

מרדכי בן ברוך טעסלער - ז' שבט תש"ג 1943

פראדיל בת שלמה טרויבכ"ץ - ר"ח ניסן 1933

הרב ר' אשר זעליג בן אריה עהרליך - כ"ו אלול תשי"ז 1957

שיינדל בת הרב ר' אהרון הכהן שאנצער - י"ד תשרי תשמ"ב 1981

Map of Romania and neighboring countries in Central and Eastern Europe

Viseu de Sus and neighboring towns, Ruscova,
Moisei, and Borsa

The engagement picture of my mother and father, Esther (Rosenfeld) and
Shloime Tessler. They were married on *Tu b'Av*, 1925.

My paternal grandmother, Fradel (Traubkatz)
Tessler, who would sit by the window reciting
Tehillim as she watched her grandchildren play
in the yard.

The *matzeiva* of my paternal grandfather, Mottel
Tessler, in the cemetery in Viseu, Romania.

My aunt, Rachel, called Rozhe-neinie. I
was named after her husband, Mendel,
and she gave me his Tefillin *Zekel* for my
Bar-Mitzva.

My first-cousin, Esther Tessler (Kopolowitz),
Rozhe-neinie's daughter, standing in front of
the well near her house. Each well served several
homes as there was no running water in Viseu.

Translation

M e d i c a l   R e p o r t

Transit Camp Hospital   Main Ledger : 667
pistol shot into the left tight   No.926

Name   : Tessler   entrance on 22 August 1945
First name   : Mende   Camp Cham
Nationality : Roumanian   moved on 28 October 1946
Birth dates : 23 October 1929   to hospital for D.P. - Munic
Place of birth: Oberwischoldesus   (political and racial perse-
Status   : unmarried   cutees)
Religion   : Jewish
Profession   : student

Relatives living at : Oberwischoldesus

Antecedents :

Has been wounded on 23.4.1945 during the hostilities by a
pistol shot into the left thigh. First treatment applied in
a hospital in Cham, Niederbayern.
Was accepted for further treatment on 24.8. by this hospital.

B. Results of examination :
a 15 years old boy of reduced "E.u.K.Z" (remark translator :
probably state of health). Very pale complexion, muscose fibres
almost bloodless. No pathologic diagnosis concerning inner
organs.

Local diagnosis :
Insensible scar of the size of a bullet, 4 fingers above the
upper edge of the patella, on the left bending side of the
upper thigh. There is an incision wound of about 5 cm on the
middle of the bending side of the left upper thigh. The muscles
of the left upper and under thigh are in a very athrophic state.
The surroundings of the incision wound are still infiltrated.
The skin is redened and there is a secretion of pus. The moving

Feldafing, 16 March 1946
     Head Physician   Section Doctor
     Dr.Sann   Dr.Zepke

21.3. The discharge of the patient proved to be impossible,
because some fresh infiltrations occurred around the scars
on the left upper thigh. In spit of putting the leg at
rest by the help of splints, a new incision had to be made
under ethyl chloride narcosis. The incision was made at
the upper and lower end of the scar. Moderate quantities

Excerpts of my medical records from Feldafing. I spent close to 4 years
in hospitals in Feldafing and Munich, from the time of my liberation in
1945 until I immigrated to America in 1949.

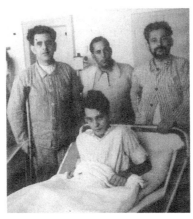

Pictures of me in the hospital surrounded by the other
patients who took care of me. I was around 16 years old, the
youngest patient there.

Photograph of me in Munich in 1947

My brothers, Tuli and Baruch, my father, and me, in Munich in 1947.

Engagement picture of Nusia (Ehrlich) and
Mendel Tessler

בעזוהי"ת

שמח תשמח חתן וכלה לפ"ק

אעלה את ירושלים על ראש שמחתי
בסימן טוב ובמזל טוב

קול ששון   וקול שמחה
קול חתן   וקול כלה

מתכבדים אנחנו להזמין את קרובינו ומיודעינו
לבוא לקחת חבל בשמחת כלולת בנינו היקרים

ה"ה הבחור החתן המופלג

כמר מנחם דוב ני"

עב"ג הכלה הבתולה המהוללה

מרת נעכא בילא תחי"

שתתקיים אי"ה בשעה טובה ומוצלחת
ביום א' פ' שלח, י"ב סיון, תשי"ד לפ"ק
למספרס 6.13
בשעה 6:30 בערב בדיוק

האטעל דיפלומאט
רחוב 43 מס' 108 וועסט
ניו יארק

ואי"ה בשמחת צאצאיכם נשיב לכם כגמולכם הטוב

אבי החתן   הורי הכלה
שלמה טעסלער ורעיתו   הרב אשר זעליג עהרליך ורעיתו

Rabbi and Mrs. Selig Ehrlich
Mr. and Mrs. Solomon Tessler

request the honour of your presence
at the marriage of their children

Nusia
to
Mendel

on Sunday, the thirteenth of June
Nineteen hundred and fifty four
at six-thirty p. m.
Hotel Diplomat
108 West 43rd Street
New York City

Brides Residence
339 Clifton Place
Brooklyn 16, N. Y.

Our wedding invitation

On our wedding day, June 13, 1954

Nusia dancing the Mitzvah-Tanz with her father, Rabbi Usher Selig Ehrlich, as her mother, Reb Sheindel Ehrlich, looks on. Her brother, Chaim, is standing behind her.

Proud new parents, Nusia and me, with our firstborn

Nusia with our three children in Crown Heights

Esther, Selig and Aron growing up, at our house in Flatbush

In my printing shop, Mendy Press Inc.

Nusia and me at various family simchas

My brothers, Tuli and Baruch, my father, and me

My brothers, Baruch, Tuli, and me

My father, R' Shloime Tessler

My father's *kever* in Kiryat Vizhnitz, in Bnei Brak, Israel. His *Matzeiva* serves also as a *Matzeiva* for my mother, Esther, and my six brothers and sisters, who perished in the gas chambers of Birkenau. May their pure and innocent *neshomos* be avenged.

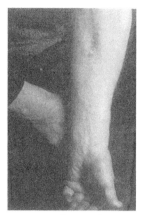

B10573 - The number tattooed on my left arm in Birkenau

My grandson, an officer in the IDF today

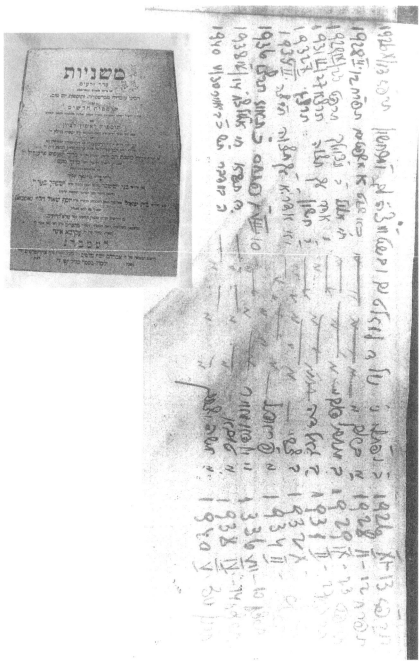

The *Mishnayos Zeroim* from Romania, found in Israel, with my father's inscription
inside listing his nine children and their birthdates.

I had this *Shivisi* plaque made to commemorate my family. It was on the *Amud* in R' Leifer's Shul for many years. The first letter of each line of the poem, written by Rabbi Eliezer Fischoff, is an acronym for Esther, my mother. The tree has 6 broken branches, representing my brothers and sisters, Goldie, Hershy, Frady, Yida Meir, Toby, and Moishy, who perished during the war. It also shows 3 tall thriving branches and they represent my brothers, Tuli and Baruch, and me, who were *zocheh* to survive and build beautiful families.

זו אחת התמונות הכי חזקות שלי מהמסע. סבי, אבא של אבא שלי, היה כאן בבירקנאו
כנער בן 15. התמונה אומרת: "היטלר, רצית וניסית להשמיד אותנו, שלא יישאר כלום מעם
ישראל. אבל אנחנו ניצחנו! מהמחנות שלך לא נשאר כלום ואילו אנחנו, עם ישראל, חזרנו
לארצנו. הקמנו מדינה. עם צבא חזק. אנחנו עדיין כאן כי יש לנו עוד מה לבשר לעולם!!!"

When my grandson visited Birkenau with his army unit, he had to submit a report
to his commanding officer describing his experience. He wrote that although the
Nazis wanted to exterminate all of *Am Yisroel* so that not even one should remain,
they were unsuccessful. Instead today their armies are gone while the Jewish
people, with the help of the *Ribono Shel Olam*, are strong, they have returned to
their homeland, they established a *medinah* with a strong army, they survived, they
rebuilt, and they will not be vanquished.

Nusia and Mendel Tessler

Nusia and me surrounded by great-grandchildren

Esther and Mutty's family

Selig and Betty's family

Ari and Naomi's family

My brother, Baruch, and me holding hands

Baruch, Tuli, and me, the three brothers together

Made in the USA
Middletown, DE
28 June 2024